RESCUED
FOR A REASON

Larry and Connie Van Oosten
As told to A. L. Rogers

RESCUED
FOR A REASON

An Unbelievable True Story

of Kidnapping, Theft, and

the Power to Overcome

Published in the United States of America by Credo House Publishers,
a division of Credo Communications LLC, Grand Rapids, Michigan
credohousepublishers.com

Scripture quotations designated NIV are from The Holy Bible, New
International Version®, NIV® Copyright ©1973, 1978, 1984, 2011 by Biblica,
Inc.® Used by permission. All rights reserved worldwide.

ISBN: 978-1-62586-193-1

Cover and interior design by Frank Gutbrod
Illustrations by Freepik.com
Editing by Donna Huisjen

Printed in the United States of America
First edition

CONTENTS

INTRODUCTION

Tuesday, February 7, 2017
3:30 a.m.

What was he thinking that morning?

In the early morning hours, a car drove up to an abandoned house. Did the driver carefully review each detail of his plan one more time? He'd been making plans for a year and a half. Now it was time to execute them. Did he go through a mental list?

Is the hammer wrapped properly? Yes. The blow to the basement window would be quieted.

Do I have the tasers? Yes. One for each of his targets, should they be necessary.

The gun? Yes.

There was more.

Sunglasses. Mask. Handcuffs. Duct tape. And much more. Each item would play an important role.

It was a short distance from the abandoned house to the home of his targets. Just a quick walk across the field. He parked his car and shut it off. The silence and darkness must have wrapped him like heavy blankets. He'd been writing his plans, in detail, for so long. He was meticulous and efficient. Having checked and double-checked every item on his list, he left the car and set out.

1

It was unusually warm for February in northwestern Illinois. During another year he might've been seen as he approached the house, a dark figure walking across the brightly reflective snow in midwinter. But on this night a fog was rolling on the warmer air, and most of the snow was gone, leaving only mud and patches of grass underfoot. It would have been easy for him to walk quietly across the dark field toward the small window at the back of the house.

Did he have his own questions that night, too?

Will breaking the glass wake them?

Do I know the layout of the house well enough to put my plans into motion?

He knelt alongside the house and pulled the hammer back. Once the glass was broken, there was no going back. A year and a half of planning hung on the next few minutes. He swung.

CRASH!

The sound of the break was muted, but there was still the clamor of glass falling to the basement floor. He listened pensively, his gun and tasers ready, should he be caught in the act. No lights turned on in the house. No noise was made in the bedroom above. It had worked just as he'd planned.

He slid himself inside. It was time to wait as his targets slept upstairs. Everything would change when the new day started.

Who was this heartless monster under the mask?

This is how it all began.

PART I

CHAPTER ONE

BOUND

The Village of Erie, Illinois, was asleep and unaware of what was happening on its outskirts. Little did its residents know or feel the dark presence of evil that hung over the small farm just outside of town.

Erie is a typical small town in the northwest corner of the state. The Mississippi River and the Iowa state line are less than a half hour to the west. Rock River, known for having once been under the purview of a young lifeguard named Ronald Reagan, is just a few miles to the east.

Erie is part of Whiteside County, only two hours straight west from the heart of Chicago, though the two couldn't be more different. The skyline is punctuated by a water tower and a grain elevator, as well as trees that are older than both of them. Rhythmic pounding of the train is the village soundtrack. The local school is known for being one of the better options in the area, drawing young families to enroll their children to become the next class of proud Erie Panthers.

Larry Van Oosten grew up in Erie and attended Western Illinois University. He met Connie during his junior year, 1969, and they later married. They eventually bought the farm his dad had farmed for fifty years. Though Connie had been raised in Chicago, she quickly acclimated to the warmth of small-town life.

After spending a few years working in a factory in Clinton, Iowa, Larry started a pest control business in Erie. He owned and operated this business for thirty years. Connie worked for the local lumberyard and later opened her own floorcovering store. As the kids grew—Amy and Jeff—Connie was approached with a job offer to be a sales rep for a carpet mill. This role would often send her out on the road for business trips. She was confident, energetic, and treated all her customers with small-town honesty. These were traits that converted many of her customers to friends. The Van Oostens retired in 2013, put their money in the bank, and got ready to enjoy a quiet life with their adult children, grandkids, and Larry's mother.

People still work hard in Erie. Friends and acquaintances still say hello on the street and at the local ball game. Families are still planted like the crops that surround them and grow in health and happiness. People trust one another; they value the small-town relationships.

Larry and Connie live in a small, two-story farmhouse on the edge of town. They have a sweeping lawn in front and some farmland out back that they lease to one of the neighbors. A large oak tree interrupts the front lawn and provides shade for their home and some protection against the winds that cross Erie's landscape. It's a quiet place to live, and they like it that way.

The Van Oostens were only a few minutes' drive from the home of their son, Jeff, and his wife, Terri. Jeff and Terri gave them three grandchildren, whom they loved to dote upon. Their daughter, Amy, lived 45 minutes away with her husband, John, in Iowa, though she still came into town at least three days a week for work at the family store. Amy and John had two children who were as doted upon by Grandma and Grandpa as the others. Along with Larry's mother, they frequently traveled to ball games and school activities. There is nothing the three seniors like better than to watch the grandkids grow.

The Van Oostens, like all families, had their trials through the years. Cancer. Heart attack. The loss of family members and close friends. Life was not always easy. There were difficult times that they were not always prepared for, but through the trials they persevered. Yet life in Erie still seemed perfect sometimes. It's the kind of place where you would just never expect certain things to happen.

Tuesday, February 7, 2017

Connie woke that morning at 7:00. This was a time that would come to mean something ominous to her from that day forward. She was lying in bed, fast asleep, when she heard yelling, and a waking nightmare began.

"Ahh!" It was Larry. *What is he yelling about*? Connie opened her eyes and looked at the clock.

7:00 a.m.

Have you ever been stuck between sleeping and dreaming? Sometimes in that in-between place nightmares can take hold. They are impossible to shake. Feelings of darkness and evil seem to wrap you tightly, frightening you, making you fear for your family, . . . yet you can't wake up.

Somehow, Larry could just sense that a man was standing over him. He opened his eyes but thought he was dreaming. A nightmare. Stuck in that in-between place.

There was indeed a man alongside his bed. He was fully dressed in black combat clothes with his face fully covered. In one hand he held a handgun; the other held something indistinguishable. To Larry, he looked like some sort of terrorist.

Why would a terrorist be in my bedroom? he wondered.

But dream states are fleeting. Awareness rushed in faster than any bullet. Larry sat bolt upright and yelled as the reality of the situation became clear. This was his worst nightmare come true. The raw fear seemed to grip him. This was *real.*

There was flash and what sounded like a shot near the foot of the bed! It wasn't the handgun. Taser wires sprung toward Larry, somehow missing him. Their long, coiled ropes lay haphazardly on the floor like a pair of snakes gone limp. He looked down and felt his chest, certain he had been shot. But there was no blood on his chest, and he felt no pain.

Have I been shot? The question barely registered in Larry's mind. It was all happening so quickly. He didn't understand. *What's going on? Was the masked man nervous? Had he shot someone before?* Larry wasn't hit, but there were drops of blood on the bed. *Where did they come from?* "Lay down on the bed!

Don't look at me." The man in the mask said flatly. In contrast to Larry's yell, the man holding the weapons spoke calmly, as though he'd done this all before.

"Lay face down," he said.

Was he nervous about what he was doing?

Still groggy from sleep, Connie tried to make sense of what she was seeing and hearing:

There was a man in their bedroom.

He was dressed entirely in black.

Combat boots.

Pants covered in pockets.

Was he military?

He was holding a taser and a handgun, pointed right at her husband.

At that moment the shock and fear were indescribable. To see a gun pointed at Larry . . . *Had he been shot? Was he bleeding? Would they live through this?*

In an instant her eyes went to his face, searching for answers but finding none. The mask that covered his head hid every identifying mark, including even his nose and mouth. He wore sunglasses to hide his eyes and a black ball cap on top of it all. A faceless intruder. *What monster was hidden behind the mask?*

"Lord, help us," she mouthed in a desperate prayer. "Please help us!"

"Where is your God now?" The man asked coldly. Something about his voice wasn't right. It was deep and mechanical, with an electronic edge. Like his mask, it hid his humanity.

"He's here. He's here with us *now*," Larry managed to assert. "He can help you. It doesn't have to be this way. We have a God who will forgive, no matter what."

"Stop talking," the garbled voice commanded.

With his handgun still pointed at Larry, he put away his taser and pulled a pair of handcuffs from a pocket by his knees. He held them out to Connie.

"Put these on him!"

The man waved his gun, directing her to Larry's side of the bed. Connie sat on the edge and tried to put handcuffs on her husband of 44 years. It was all so overwhelming, so terrifying. *This can't be real!*

He pulled shackles from another pocket and put them around Larry's ankles. Larry would not be able to run if they tried to escape. And as Connie wrestled with the cuffs, the man pulled out a roll of duct tape and begin ripping it into strips. He stood behind her, methodically placing the strips of tape on her back so they would be easy to grab and use. But for what, Connie could only guess.

Shortly after his command to cuff her husband, Connie realized she had a problem. The handcuffs didn't fit Larry's large wrists. She obediently tried to cuff her husband, but in spite of her struggles she could not make them lock. They were just too small. What would the intruder do if she couldn't get the cuffs on, as he demanded?

Connie noticed blood on Larry's back. Larry had been sleeping, as he often did, in just his boxer shorts. But red spots of blood were easily visible on his bare back, on his legs, and on their bed sheets. *Where did the blood come from? Was it Larry's?*

What had happened to him?

The man watched her in cool silence, keeping his gun trained on her just within the range of her peripheral vision. He seemed mechanical as he held her at gunpoint. Not nervous or under pressure, but confident, as though he were used to threatening people's lives. If there was any chink in his cold armor, it was that he seemed intimidated by Larry's size and strength. What would this man be willing to do if she couldn't get the cuffs on? Shoot them both, right there in the bedroom? She tried to close the handcuffs one more time, but they wouldn't budge. She had to speak to their captor.

"They don't fit."

After a long moment, the masked man relented and finally gave her another pair of handcuffs. This pair fit, and Connie heard the metal lock click into place. Larry Van Oosten, a man who prides himself on caring for those he loves, was bound with hands behind his back, his feet shackled at the ankles, and lying face down on the bed. Then the man took a strip of duct tape and covered Larry's eyes. A second strip was put over his mouth.

"I have a hard time breathing," Larry said just before the second piece was put over his mouth. This was true—Larry couldn't breathe through his nose. Fortunately, this intruder believed him and loosened the tape around Larry's mouth, allowing in a small flow of air.

Then he turned to Connie.

After using Connie to secure her husband, he instructed, "Lay face down." She lay down next to her husband, terrified of what might happen. He pulled her hands behind her back. The cold metal of handcuffs closed on her wrists, and the same telltale click of the lock seemed to echo in their bedroom. Strips of duct tape were placed over her eyes and across her mouth.

They had been asleep just minutes before. It had been like any other morning—eyes closed and lying quietly in bed. But suddenly they were at the mercy of a madman in their own bedroom, blindfolded and bound, lying helpless and speechless. They couldn't see or move. There was no one around to help and no way for them to make contact.

After he was finished binding Connie, the masked man left the room. Now that his targets had been bound, it was time for him to put the next phase of his plan into motion.

Larry and Connie lay quietly on their bed. They could hear the familiar sounds of their house as the intruder walked through it. There was the creak of the attic steps. The swing of the door to the room across the hall. The scrape of his boots on the kitchen floor. They could hear him moving all over the house. Was he stealing things? Or looking for something? They didn't know. Then it became quiet—almost eerily so.

As they listened, Larry started to turn his head back and forth, little by little loosening the tape across his mouth and eyes by rubbing it against the mattress. Slits of the morning light started to appear. He could feel that Connie was doing the same thing next to him on the bed.

Over the next several minutes they heard nothing in the house and whispered desperate questions to each other.

Is he going to kill us?

Is he coming back?

What if there's more than one person?

There were no answers to any of these questions. The silence and uncertainty were as suffocating as the duct tape.

"We're going to pray now," Larry whispered to his wife. It was all he could think of after all the questions. "Are you ready? Are you ready to meet Jesus?" He still couldn't see her, but he heard the woman he'd pledged his life to whisper "yes."

"Dear God. Please prepare us for this," Larry whispered. "We're ready. We're ready to meet you if that's what's going to happen. Please prepare us for whatever comes next."

Connie felt a certain *calm* that was hard to describe. She was still frightened, and yet she felt assured she would somehow be able to face whatever came next. She had been certain when the man had told them to lie facedown on the bed that he would kill them. The idea that something this evil, this cold, and this calculating was actually happening seemed unimaginable. But somehow, Connie was given the strength to persevere . . . to meet whatever this evil person had planned for them.

For Larry the peace felt like an irrational lack of fear, despite the reality that the man in their house was a picture of pure evil. No doubt about it. Larry could just *feel it* when he was in the room.

The Van Oostens heard their captor in the house again. Had he left and come back? They couldn't know. Larry assumed the man was going to steal their possessions and then probably kill them. That's when something happened that shook him to his core, threatening the spiritual peace that the prayer time had just ushered in. The masked man took Connie from the room.

"Don't hurt her! Please don't hurt her!" Larry yelled, helpless from his spot on the bed.

The man said nothing but pulled Connie up and pushed her into the hallway. Larry was left alone to wonder what was going to happen to his wife.

CHAPTER TWO

TAKEN

Once they were in the hallway, the masked man pulled the duct tape from Connie's eyes. He moved without empathy or emotion. He was neither malicious nor compassionate. It was as though everything he did had been preprogrammed. As though ripping duct tape off someone's skin was as routine as sending an email. With his gun pointed at her, he directed Connie to the first floor without saying anything. The quiet, methodical way he went about his tasks was unnerving.

"Close the blinds," he said mechanically after they had reached the bottom of the staircase. Connie did as she was directed, closing the blinds in their dining room and office, both of which faced the front yard. He pointed toward the desk in the office, and she sat in the familiar chair. He threw down a pad of paper and a pen. Connie started to look toward him, uncertain of what she was supposed to do.

"Don't ever look at me," he commanded. She focused quickly on the paper again. He made sure she could see his gun in the corner of her vision.

15

"Write down your financial information. I want every account number, and I want to know how much is in them. Write down the name of each bank. I want to know anywhere that you have money."

So, this is all about money. Connie started to write. All their hard work and savings. All their plans for retirement.

As she wrote, Connie decided she wouldn't give him every piece of information. She gave him some. She wrote down account numbers and the name of their bank. But she counted on this intruder not knowing all that they had or being able to guess that she was holding back information.

When she was finished writing, the man started to ask questions in his flat, methodical delivery style. As though all of this were perfectly normal.

"Where are your cell phones?" Connie told him, and he took them.

"Which rooms have land lines?" She told him that, too.

"What are your email addresses and passwords?" He wrote down her answers on a piece of paper and put it into one of his pockets.

"Is anyone coming by the house today?" Connie thought for a minute. They were in the middle of renovating the basement.

"Our carpet layer. He's supposed to come later this morning." The man texted him on her phone, telling him not to come.

"Do you have property besides this house? I want access to it."

"No. Not really." They had a place up north, but it could be entered only with a coded key card. Was he thinking he would escape there? It was at a resort. You couldn't just go there unannounced and hide away. There was no key she could have given him.

"Bring me your billfolds and any money you have in the house."

When she returned, he produced some financial papers that were already drawn up and ready for her to sign. He waved his gun, reminding her in a silent way of what would happen if she didn't comply. Connie didn't really look at them. One looked as though it might have been a promissory note. One looked like a transfer to First Trust and Savings Bank, where they had an account, but she wasn't sure exactly. She didn't read them but just did as she was told. They were clearly a part of his sinister plan. He told her this was his job, that he was part of a large organization that traveled the Midwest in search of people like themselves; they kidnapped them and took their money. He would keep them for two weeks, take their money, and then he would have to kill them.

When they were finished, he picked up the papers and used his gun to direct her toward the stairs. Back in the bedroom, the man directed Connie to release Larry from his cuffs so he could sign the papers too, continuing to point the gun at them.

"What is it?" Larry asked.

"I don't know," was all she could say. Connie held the documents while Larry signed. Then she had to cuff him again.

How long was this going to go on? Would this be enough for him? Would they be released, or was he going to shoot?

The man cuffed Connie's hands behind her back again, covered her eyes and mouth with more duct tape, and had her lie back down on the bed.

"You won't be harmed as long as you do what you're told," he announced before leaving the room. At least twenty minutes passed before he returned again. What was he doing? Was he looting their home? Connie and Larry could do nothing but wait and see what transpired.

When he returned, he took Connie from the room a second time. "Don't hurt her!" Larry yelled again, feeling totally helpless as she was marched from the room.

"Can I please use the restroom?" she asked before he forced her down the stairs again. Nausea threatened to overtake her. She felt so helpless. So broken. The man nodded yes.

Everything they were experiencing was bizarre and terrifying. Yet the unique sense of calm, of God watching over them, remained with Connie. She was frightened, but able to continue on with whatever was going to happen. When she was finished in the bathroom, the man waved his gun to get her to move downstairs.

There was mud all over the floor in the house. His footprints were everywhere. He handed her a rag.

"Clean it up."

Connie got some cleaning supplies from the kitchen and then dropped down on her hands and knees, starting to clean up the evidence. He stood behind her with his gun as she worked to hide his crimes. He was doing everything he could to degrade, humiliate, and control her. He seemed to be thinking, *I am in control; I can make them do anything I want.*

After she was finished, he instructed her to sit in their family room and reattached the handcuffs, this time in front of her. He put duct tape over her eyes.

"Don't move," he ordered before going back upstairs.
Please, God. Deliver us.

Larry realized the masked man had returned to their bedroom. He pulled him from the bed and directed him toward the hallway and the staircase beyond.

"I'm taking you to another location," the man volunteered.

"What do you mean, we're going to another location?" Larry asked, but the man would not answer. Larry wanted to fight back, but he was reluctant to try anything. Surely they'd be shot if he did so. In order to keep Connie safe, he suppressed the urge to fight.

The trip down the stairs was a struggle. Larry couldn't see because of the duct tape and could hardly move his legs because of the shackles. When they finally made it downstairs, the man led Larry into their attached two-stall garage and ushered him toward the trunk of a car. He told Larry to climb inside, but the leg shackles made this impossible. After the masked man released them, Larry did as he was told. It felt like a big trunk, and even though he couldn't see anything, he was sure it was not the trunk to one of their cars. Connie was brought out next and forced inside the same trunk. Then the lid slammed. Everything went dark. Even with the tape still on their eyes, they could tell that all light was gone. What inhumane treatment would come next?

Around 8:00 a.m.

The car started and pulled out. Exhaust fumes started to seep into the trunk. Alone in the dark, they could easily have pulled the duct tape away from their mouths and eyes. But Larry and Connie decided to only loosen the tape so they could see under it and whisper to each other. They were too afraid to do more than that. Too afraid to yell or talk loudly. Who knew what their captor might do?

The car stopped after only a short distance. They could see almost nothing in the dark trunk, but after a few minutes they heard the sounds of him turning a screwdriver. He was working on something at the back of the car.

"What's he doing?" Connie asked.

"I think he's switching the license plate."

Why was he doing this? And where on earth were they going? Connie and Larry could only wait and pray.

Though it was an unusually warm day for February in Illinois, a cold uncertainty was seeping into every part of their bodies, and they shivered in the trunk. They were traveling in the clothes they had slept in. A pair of plaid boxer shorts was all that Larry was wearing. Connie was in an oversized, white, long-sleeved t-shirt, with black pajama pants and a pair of socks.

Every indignity, every malicious act—from invading their home to threatening them at gunpoint to forcing them to travel bound up in a trunk while wearing only sleepwear in the winter—showed them something about this man. *What was he capable of? How far would he go?* Whoever he was, they knew he was not sympathetic to anything they might be feeling.

More light appeared as they traveled. The car was rusty. Holes in the floor allowed them to glimpse bits of the road. The masked man, now their kidnapper, drove for what they felt to be quite some time. It was impossible to know exactly how far from home they had traveled or how long they had been in the trunk. The car turned and moved in different directions. At different points they felt speed bumps, but nothing indicated clearly where he'd taken them.

"Where could this be?" Connie wondered aloud, but neither could guess.

When the car finally parked, the man opened the lid and forced the Van Oostens to climb out. They both had tape covering their eyes, but he didn't seem to care how difficult exiting the trunk was for them. Connie had arthritis, was handcuffed, and was without shoes. Larry, though not hampered by arthritis, was not much better off. It was an awkward, difficult process, yet the masked man forced them to get out one at a time, pulling them in his impatience. Another malicious indignity.

He led them through a garage and into what seemed to be a small house. Connie and Larry were each trying to see under the tape and catch a glimpse of their surroundings, but they couldn't make out much. Once inside, he led them one at a time to an open closet. There was a secret opening in the floor, a square hole three and a half feet on each side. A door was swung back on open hinges. One at a time, they were forced down a ladder and into a small room. Wherever they were about to go wasn't a random hole in the ground. It was a cell intentionally built for the purpose of hiding someone. Their captivity had been planned. *But why?*

What was down there? Was it a basement of some kind? Were there more men in masks? More guns? Would they ever escape from here alive? Larry and Connie had no idea. All they really knew was that this was no ordinary basement.

CHAPTER THREE

THE SECRET ROOM

The man led each of the Van Oostens, one at a time, to metal barn door handles that had been mounted to the cement wall. The two handles were about six feet apart. Larry was cuffed to one and Connie to the other. Connie was closer to the ladder. They stood quietly, still with duct tape over their eyes and able to see very little of the room. Just when they thought things couldn't get any more bizarre, they realized the nightmare would not be over any time soon.

"We will see everything you do," their captor informed them. "Don't try anything. Don't *dare* touch anything. Don't *break* anything. We are watching you."

They listened quietly, afraid of what might happen if they spoke out.

"Do not shout or make noise. Do not attempt to call for help," he warned them ominously. "We will hear everything you say to each other."

Without further discussion, the man left. They heard the ladder being pulled up to the main floor and the secret door swinging closed. The padlock clicked into place.

Time started to pass slowly. Silent minutes stretched into hours. Larry's bare feet grew cold and tired on the cement floor. Connie's socked feet felt the same. They couldn't sit or lie down. At some point during the long wait Larry loosened the tape. Connie eventually did the same. They could see each other at least, but it was a small relief. Anything they said would be heard. Bound by their handcuffs, and unwilling to speak above short whispers, they took a look around the room. Perhaps they could find a clue as to where they had been taken.

Small red lights caught their eyes. They realized there were cameras in each of the four corners. The lenses were trained on them. These tireless lights were silent reminders that their every move was being watched.

There was also a microphone attached to one wall. Their captors were watching and listening, . . . for now.

A mattress was on the floor in the corner. It seemed out of place. It was covered with a bedspread. Pillows were placed at the head of the bed, as though someone had tried to decorate for them. The sheets, pillows, and bedspread all matched. Someone had gone to some length to decorate the room. *But why?*

There was also a big-screen TV on the wall. A stack of books. Andy Griffith video tapes. There was even a small Bible. In one corner there was a sink, a shower and tub, and a commode. Nothing seemed right.

Two matching stacks of food occupied another corner. Perhaps one was for Larry and one for Connie? There were boxes of granola bars and packages of Ramen noodles. There were pudding cups and bottled water. Every item was stacked neatly— too neatly. Something about how carefully it had all been placed there was unnerving.

What was this place?

They could do nothing to free themselves or stop this madness without alerting their captors. They just had to wait for whatever would come next.

Hours passed slowly. Larry and Connie could only guess at what time it was. They grew cold. Like many basements, this secret room wasn't heated for a winter in the Midwest. Even if it had been heated, their sparse sleep clothes wouldn't have been enough to keep them warm. Connie moved her feet as far as she could stretch and pulled the blanket off the bed with her toes. At least they were close enough to share the edges and maybe gain a little warmth.

The passing hours sapped them of their strength. Everything that had happened that morning was taking its toll. The shock of their captor's appearance and demands. The stress of being under constant threat. The rush of adrenaline. It was all ebbing into a tide of fear and exhaustion, threatening to overcome them. Lack of food and being forced to stand made Connie feel weak and woozy. As the day prolonged, she couldn't take it anymore. Connie let her legs go slack and hung from the handcuff by her wrist, just to give her body some respite. It hurt to do so, as the unforgiving metal pressed into her flesh, but she was just so tired. There were no other options.

How long is this going to go on?

When the man finally returned hours later, he descended into the room. Still threatening them with his gun, he unhandcuffed Connie, ignoring the bruises growing on her wrist. He did not look at Larry.

"Where are you taking her?" Larry asked desperately. "I said, where are you taking her?" The man did not respond. But he indicated that she was to move toward the ladder.

"No! Don't hurt her! Please don't hurt her."

Avoiding any contact with Larry, he made Connie climb the ladder to the first story, directing her toward an empty room upstairs. She sat on the floor. The room had some tools and boards in it, as though someone had been doing a remodel. The windows were also covered, leaving no chance to see where they were. Connie guessed it would've been someone's bedroom under normal conditions.

"Do as I say, and you and your family will be safe," he told her. "Keep your head down and don't ever look at me." He held the gun at just the right height so Connie could always see it out of the corner of her eye.

My family? I thought. *I've got to do what he says, or he'll hurt the kids.* The indescribable feeling of peace and calm returned. She and Larry might not make it out of this, but Connie knew she had to keep it together to protect her family. She spoke calmly to her captor from her spot on the floor.

"How can you do this? Don't you have family? Don't you have people you care about? How can you do this to us and our family?"

The man remained quiet. Had she just signed her own death warrant? But, instead, he simply produced her cell phone, as though he were taking care of an everyday task. It was time to put the next phase of his plan into action. With his voice modulator on and his characteristic flat delivery, he asked, "Who expects to see you today?"

Iowa

Amy was with her nine-year-old son in their school gymnasium. They were about to watch her fourteen-year-old daughter play a late afternoon basketball game. John was still at work and would have to miss this one, but Larry and Connie were supposed to be there to cheer on their granddaughter. It is only about a 45-minute drive to the game. Not too far for loving grandparents to be involved in their grandkids' lives. Then Amy's phone rang.

"We won't be at the game tonight," Connie said flatly. "We were finishing up the basement and lost track of time." She tried to focus on the floor rather than pay attention to the gun in her peripheral vision. If she could just hold her voice steady, she could get through this and hang up, keeping her family from danger.

"Okay. No problem," Amy responded.

Connie ended the call quickly. No extended chitchat that might have revealed the stress in her voice. Amy didn't think much of it. It wasn't like her parents to miss one of their grandkids' games. At the same time, Amy had no reason to doubt her mom. The gymnasium was noisy with people finding their spots in the bleachers and the basketball teams warming up. Amy picked out some seats with her son and let her concerns go with the sound of the buzzer. She'd talk with her mom again tomorrow.

Larry and Connie were also scheduled to pick up Larry's mother and take her to the game. The 89-year-old didn't use text messaging, so Connie had to call her, too.

"We won't be coming by after all," she said, trying again to sound convincing. His mom didn't let the conversation end as quickly as Connie wanted. After all, she *loved* attending her great grandchildren's events.

"Oh, I had my coat on and was ready to leave," she objected.

After a few strained minutes, Connie was able to hang up.

"Who else?" the man asked.

"Larry has coffee every Wednesday with his friends, Jim and Kathy." Their weekly coffee meetings had been taking place for more than twenty years. It was out of the ordinary for Larry to miss. The masked man pulled out Larry's phone and quickly texted Jim. Coffee was canceled.

Other events were canceled. too. The man sent a text to Connie's hairdresser canceling a hair appointment. He also sent a text to the carpet layer, who was due to return that week.

The man's meticulous plan continued being put into action.

Keeping his gun trained on Connie, he directed her back down the ladder. Handing her the key for Larry's cuffs, he allowed her to unhook her husband so they could both go to bed for the night. She was to lay the key on the stack of books.

At this point Connie noticed that their captor didn't seem to want to speak to Larry. He wouldn't get near him and seemed to keep his distance. Why? He'd spoken to Larry at their home. He'd stood close to him as he'd bound them both and even forced Larry into the car. Why was he keeping his distance now? Even with all the compounding abnormalities of this day, this seemed strange.

The man kept the gun trained on both of them. Any attempt to rush him, tackle him, or otherwise fight back could have ended with a bullet landing in one or both of them. They had no choice but to comply with his demands. He ascended the ladder and closed the door. They heard the lock click into place again and realized he was leaving them for the night.

What now? Were they supposed to get comfortable here? After being taken from their home and handcuffed all day, were they expected to relax and watch Andy Griffith? Or get lost in a good book before turning in for the night? Their cuffs hung grimly on the wall, reminders of what was really happening in this room.

Before lying down, Larry decided to open up the Bible they had found. The print in the Bible was too small for Larry to read, but a familiar passage came to mind, one that Larry had heard and read numerous times.

"And we know that in all things God works for the good of those who love him, who have been called according to his purpose." (Romans 8:28)

He prayed that this would be true in their lives and that God would work something good out of this situation.

They spoke very little. Reluctantly, they decided to try to sleep, though no real sleep would come that night. They held on to one another for warmth and encouragement. They were constantly on the alert, always listening for the sound of their captor's boots on the floor above. Connie lay awake all night, listening specifically for the noise of footsteps. The stress was overwhelming. *How long could they last like this?*

CHAPTER FOUR

INCREASING DEMANDS

Wednesday, February 8, 2017
The kidnapper's house

Morning broke, but their stress did not. Neither Larry nor Connie felt rested. They'd been held against their wills for over 24 hours. *Did anyone know yet? Had Connie's story been good enough to fool her family yesterday? When would people discover that they were missing? Would the police get involved?*

They finally heard the sounds they'd been waiting for. Footsteps on the main floor told them their kidnapper had returned. *What would happen now? Would they live through the day?* There were so many questions without answers. All they could do was wait. His voice suddenly came over the speaker.

"Put the cuffs on."

A minute later and he was coming down the ladder. The temperature seemed to drop as he descended. He was still wearing his terrorist, military-like garb with his face fully masked and a gun pointed at them. Connie was released and given one of Larry's coats and a pair of boots. The kidnapper must've taken

31

the clothing while he had been in their house. Connie was to be taken upstairs. Larry would have to stand alone and wait.

On her way to the ladder, Connie passed out. She and Larry hadn't eaten anything or had anything to drink from the room's stash. It was Wednesday morning, and they hadn't eaten a bite since Monday before going to bed. The fearful night of listening for their captors had only made the situation worse.

Connie fell as everything went black. Larry couldn't catch her from his spot, handcuffed as he was to the wall. The kidnapper just watched her crumble. Fortunately, she'd fallen as she was walking across the mattress on the floor and was not injured. After coming to, she required a minute to gather herself before eating a granola bar, but she wasn't feeling well. She forced herself to move toward the ladder. The trauma of the last 24 hours was starting to have an effect. Unsympathetic, the man waved at the ladder with his gun.

"Don't hurt her!" Larry begged again, unable to do anything to help his wife. "Please. Don't hurt her."

The man touched the switch on his voice modulator. "If you do as I say, nothing will happen to you. I'm just going to keep you for a couple days; then you can go back home." This provided little comfort to either of the Van Oostens.

As Connie used the restroom upstairs, the man threw jeans and a sweatshirt down to Larry. He would have to wait until he was released to finally be able to put these on.

The man then directed Connie to the same bedroom they had occupied the day before. She was again forced to sit on the floor and keep her head down while he stood nearby with his gun just within her range of vision. It was time to make a few more phone calls, requesting that monies be transferred to one account and a check be drawn up in the name of a company the masked man would supply.

They would also have to call or text anyone who might be expecting them that day.

I've got to do this, Connie thought. *I've got to do this to protect Larry and the kids.* Connie dialed Amy's number.

Amy started to suspect that something wasn't right after a second quick conversation with her mom in two days. Something was definitely going on.

That's really weird. Why did they leave town? Did something happen with one of my grandparents and they just didn't want to say anything right away? Maybe there's something going on with the family and they don't want me to know about it yet.

Amy reasoned that she would find out after her parents got to wherever they were going. She never assumed anything criminal was happening. *Why would it have been?*

One of the most important calls to make was to the Van Oostens' primary bank in Erie, Illinois. Their captor had specific instructions for Connie, things she had to request and things she needed to initiate in order for her to make a large withdrawal from their accounts. If she did not, the captor made clear, then not only *her* life but also the lives of her children and grandchildren would be in danger. The masked man made sure she understood that.

He wanted to know how much money was available to him. Connie had a good guess, but he wanted an *exact* number. She called First Trust and Savings Bank in Erie, placed the phone on speaker, and laid it on the floor so the man could hear the whole conversation. But surprisingly, the woman at the bank could not give Connie a straight answer. It was not long before the man became so frustrated that he grabbed the phone and hung up.

"You've got to figure this out," he commanded. "Call back."

Connie called again. The same woman answered. Despite Connie's careful questions, they couldn't figure out exactly how much money the Van Oostens had available. The man's frustrations grew, and he hung up again.

Over and over this happened, six or seven times. Connie obediently did as she was commanded, calling the bank with specific questions and instructions about their account. The same teller would answer her calls but then be unable to provide the answers she needed. The teller seemed confused for some reason. How come she couldn't answer an account holder's questions? The masked man grew more and more agitated, repeatedly grabbing the phone from the floor and hanging it up in anger. He started waving his gun more wildly, losing the cold, mechanical demeanor he'd adopted up until that point. Evidently he hadn't planned on this.

"I can't believe how patient you are with her," the man remarked at one point.

What am I supposed to do? What choice do I have? Connie thought. *You have a gun on me.*

After so many unsuccessful attempts, the man seemed to be reaching a breaking point.

"Figure this out!" he demanded. He pointed the gun at Connie again with a renewed sense of gravity. "Try again."

God had given Connie an unexplainable peace. She knew that if she got hysterical or started crying, this was *not* going to go well.

"I think it might be better if we just talk to Mark Hanson," Connie said. "Larry has been working with him for years. He will have the information you want. He's at a different branch, but I think that would be the best way to go."

Using Connie's phone and her name, the man started sending emails to Mark Hanson, the president and CEO of First Trust and Savings Bank.

Eventually, the abductor was able to learn exactly how much money they had access to, the full balance amount of their accounts. He had already made Connie and Larry sign papers at the house requesting wire transfers and withdrawals. The pieces of his plan appeared to be starting to come together. Just a few more details to take care of. From another room upstairs, one that included the monitors showing the basement room where Larry and Connie had been held, he sent another email to Mark Hanson, again posing as Larry. The process for making a large withdrawal was started. Soon he would have the money in hand.

An amount totaling $350,000.

For now, he would return Connie to her spot in the basement. A few hours, and he could put the next part of the plan into action.

It was late in the afternoon when the hidden door was opened again. The masked man dropped the ladder down and ordered Connie to climb up. He didn't make her handcuff Larry to the wall this time but kept the gun pointed at her, always threatening to bring things to a bloody conclusion if they tried anything.

"Please! Please! Don't hurt my wife. Please don't hurt her," Larry begged again. The feeling of helplessness as he just stood there was soul-crushing. He would have done *anything* to protect his wife. But if he rushed their abductor, he might kill her.

The man ignored Larry but said coldly again to Connie. "If you do what I say, you'll be fine. Go."

As though all of this is no big deal! Connie thought. *As though kidnapping them, stealing their savings, and threatening their lives was absolutely nothing out of the ordinary.*

It was all so strange. The man was so methodical, as though this were just another day of work for him. He seemed to lack any empathy over what he was putting them through.

"We are going to the bank to withdraw the money."

Connie was surprised. "I can't go anywhere looking like this."

She was still in her pajamas, without sleep, nutrition, makeup, or a shower. On a typical day she would never leave the house without makeup on and her hair done. Connie couldn't imagine that anyone would think she looked normal. The man seemed to be considering what she was saying. He pulled out her purse and handed it to her.

"Go do what you can." He indicated that she could go to the bathroom. Inside the purse was a comb and an eyebrow pencil. Not much to work with. The bathroom also did not have lights. Water wouldn't come from the faucets, either. Yet there was water on the floor. Her socks were soaked by the time she was through.

He didn't produce any new clothes for Connie but handed her a pair of boots, Larry's socks, and one of Larry's coats. There was no talking or explanation. She could only guess at when he might have taken these items from their home.

She slid her feet into the boots, dreading what was coming.

Do I have the strength for this? She could see the gun in her peripheral vision. It was always, always, always pointed in her direction.

"Just make sure to do everything I say, and no one is going to get hurt."

CHAPTER FIVE

THE BANK

Albany, Illinois

For the first time since they had been taken captive, the kidnapper was no longer wearing his facemask. Instead he wore a wig, a pair of sunglasses, and a hat to hide his identity. A brown beard with gray speckling the edges covered the rest of his face. His voice modulator was still strapped around his neck, the small black microphone hidden by his beard.

He directed Connie to keep her head down and the tape over her eyes and to avoid looking at him. She climbed into the back seat of an aging Chevrolet Caprice. At least she wouldn't have to ride in the trunk this time. He handed her a pair of sunglasses to cover the tape over her eyes. Her captor must have hoped this would hide the fact that she was being held against her will.

"Don't look at me and keep the tape on," he said as they drove. Connie was concerned as to how many others were still at the house, and what they might do to Larry if she were to disobey any of the orders given to her.

It was sometime after 4:00 p.m. on Wednesday, February 8, when they left the location of their captivity. They arrived about forty minutes later in Albany, Illinois, where Mark Hanson had an office at the Albany branch of First Trust and Savings Bank. During the drive the man would have Connie call the bank once more, to ensure that they would still see her that late in the day.

"*You* will have to go into the bank to get the money," he announced. "Everything is ready."

He parked on a small incline about one and a half blocks from the bank, just down the main street. Connie felt the car stop and wondered again if she would have the strength to do what he required. She removed the duct tape and put the sunglasses back on. They were in Albany, alright. She recognized the town. They were only twenty minutes from Erie. From home.

Can I really keep up the lie that everything is okay with the bank employees? What will happen to Larry if I don't?

Her stomach turned. She didn't feel well at all. Everything she'd experienced was taking a physical toll. But she knew her family's safety was at stake. If she didn't perform, one of the others might injure or kill Larry, or they might go after Amy's or Jeff's family. Somehow, each time she thought of these possibilities, that indescribable feeling of strength and determination came over her, enabling her to do what she must in order to keep her husband and family safe. She just had to do it—just get through it—to bring this nightmare to an end.

"Call them," he demanded, handing Connie her cell phone. It was almost closing time. He wanted to make sure the bank employees would meet with her before letting Connie out of the car.

Connie spoke with someone who said the late meeting would be fine. Her captor told her to go, putting her purse in her hands.

He gave me a piece of paper with a name on it. "Have them make a check out to this name and bring the check and this piece of paper back with you."

She tried to open the door on her side of the back seat, but it was stuck, forcing her to exit on the traffic side, which was right behind him. "Look straight ahead," he told her as she exited the vehicle.

By the time Connie walked up the block to the bank, it was closed for the day, but an employee opened the door and let her inside. First Trust and Savings Bank is a small building with arched windows and a red brick exterior. It sits kitty-corner from the Albany Public Library, a matching brick building in a friendly community. Not the kind of place you would expect a major crime to be carried out. Yet as soon as she entered, Connie began to look around the room for anyone who might look out of place, possibly someone working with the kidnapper, making certain that she did what she was told. She knew it was likely that someone else in the building was working with her captor and would be watching her movements. She just didn't know who. There was somebody talking to one of the tellers and various employees in the offices surrounding the lobby. Another customer was still talking with someone. There was even a man who walked up to the drive-up window, which was not normal. If their captor were part of a bigger group that staged kidnappings and theft across the country, they were probably good at what they did. There was no guaranteeing she would be able to spot them.

But Connie didn't have the time to decide whether any of them looked suspicious. She was shown into an office, where she met with the branch manager, Patty Hoogheem. Patty had papers for Connie to sign, which would complete the withdrawal of her money.

Deciding this was her chance to get a better look around the bank, Connie made a simple request.

"May I use the restroom?"

"Sure." Patty pointed her in the right direction.

Perhaps this diversion would allow her to see whether anything looked strange or out of place.

In the bathroom Connie decided she would write a note to Patty, explaining her plight. She couldn't just say something out loud. There might be others in the building listening in on their conversation. But if she could slide a note to her, then maybe she could get help. This could be the last chance to notify someone and get help. *Who knew what would happen once they had the money? At the same time, what if writing the note was the exact thing that would get Larry killed?*

It was a desperate plan, but it was the only option Connie had to safely alert someone, *anyone,* without risking discovery. She walked back to Patty's office.

She looked in her purse for something to write on. As before, there wasn't much of anything inside. Someone had emptied it of most of its usual contents. The comb. The eyebrow pencil. But then in the bottom of her purse she found something that must've been forgotten, a church bulletin.

This could be our only chance at anybody even knowing what's happening to us.

Connie scratched out a note on the bulletin: "My husband and I are being held at gunpoint. Do not react. Do not follow us."

She hoped and prayed it wouldn't get them into more trouble. Connie slid the note across the desk to Patty with the financial documents signed and ready. All her hopes rested on this note. How would Patty react?

Patty read the note.

"Don't react," Connie said very quietly. "I'm being watched." Patty looked up quietly and excused herself from the office, taking the note with her. Connie would have to wait and wonder if she had just sealed her fate.

At this point it was well after 5:00 p.m. Central Time. The bank was officially closed, though another customer was still inside. Someone else also walked up to the drive-up window outside, which, again, was unusual. Everything seemed suspicious. *Were her captors keeping an eye on her?* Connie could feel the fear rising in her. She just didn't know whether or not they were being watched. *How big was this group? How many were nearby?*

Mark Hanson knew Larry Van Oosten to be a friendly, professional businessman. He'd managed his account for several years and had enjoyed the work. In many ways, Larry was a model customer. He didn't know Connie, as he had always worked with Larry alone. The direct and somewhat demanding emails he'd received from him the night before had seemed a little strange—the tone of the requests didn't match his cordial relationship with Larry—but he had done his part with the paperwork and put it out of his mind.

Mark was finishing up a meeting with another customer in his office when Patty called him and asked him to meet her in the back of the bank.

This can't be good, Mark thought. *It's unusual to request a meeting in the back of the bank.*

Patty handed him a note. He could immediately tell by the handwriting that the person who had written it was distressed.

"She told me that she's being watched by her kidnappers," Patty said.

Mark decided this threat had to be real. If it wasn't, they at least had to check and know for sure. "Let's just play it cool," he said, and the two went back to the office where Connie waited.

Even after hours spent shackled to a wall, after hours spent with a gun pointed at her and threats made against her family, Connie Van Oosten was still able to do what she needed to in order to get through this horrible nightmare. Yet Mark could see by the stress in her eyes and the disheveled state of her clothes and hair that something was clearly amiss.

"Just keep looking straight ahead. Act normal," Mark said. "I need some answers as soon as possible to help you. To give you the best shot."

As the three began to talk, Mark and Patty realized how little Connie knew. She didn't know who was holding them captive or where they were being held. She also didn't know what type of car she'd ridden in to get there. However, she knew that she'd been dropped off just south of the bank.

Unbeknownst to Connie or her captor, the bank had been robbed a few months earlier. New cameras had been installed after the robbery, some of which pointed to the south, where Connie said the car was parked.

Do we already have the car on film? Mark wondered. *Perhaps we could track the license plate number.*

But they couldn't check that footage immediately. Not without drawing unwanted attention. Something more had to be done.

Mark decided to call a friend, a former police officer who lived across the street from the bank. He reasoned that his friend could go out for a walk and let Mark know if he saw anyone suspicious in the street, perhaps someone waiting in a car. Ideally, this friend would be able to get the license plate number for the vehicle.

He placed a call in an open office next door, so it wouldn't look to anyone who might be watching as though he were helping Connie. He discovered that his friend had just recently moved and was no longer in the area.

"Is there anything you can do? Anyone you could call?"

"I'm sorry," his friend replied.

"We've got to help these people," Mark said. "We've got to *do* something."

"This is above my pay grade," the former officer said. Connie was shocked to overhear this. It was overwhelming to know that a former law officer was unwilling to help someone in danger! She felt so helpless. *Who would help them get out of this?* she wondered. *Why didn't they call their close family friend, the local police chief, Wyatt Heywaert?*

Alarmed and angry, Connie resolved to just get out of the bank and get the check to her captors. This was all taking way too long. The longer she took in the bank, the more likely it was that they would become suspicious and do something to Larry.

Hanson was shocked by that comment, too.

"I don't care! Somebody's got to help. I'm going out the side door, and I'm going to follow him." Mark came back into the office with Patty and Connie.

"Please, you have to be so careful," Connie said urgently. "Don't look out the window. He might see. They still have Larry. I just have to do this."

"But we've got to do something," Mark said. "At least stay in the bank. Don't go back there."

"We can't take a chance like that," Connie told him. Despite his protests, Connie knew she had to finish her captor's plan, and quickly. She wouldn't do anything that might make them hurt Larry, or worse.

Still angry at the gentleman on the phone, she went into action. "I can't take any more time. I have to go." She put the check into her purse.

Mark and Patty reluctantly agreed. They decided that Patty would walk her to the front door and unlock it for her. Connie told Patty, "Just don't look at the car. Just pretend like you're saying goodbye to me. Please don't look at the car and act as though you know anything." Patty nodded.

"There's no expert or hotline for this," Mark would say later. "We didn't want to call the police, because if a squad car showed up at the bank, then Larry would be dead. We just hoped that if we could get these guys the money, we would be buying time."

How many more kidnappers were watching them? Who on the street might be working with their captor? They could only guess. Together the two women went through the front doors. Patty waved as Connie walked toward an old car.

Connie got in and gave her captor the envelope as he quickly backed out of his spot. A check for $350,000 made out to Store Edge LLC.

Across the road was a gas station named Kelly's. Connie did not yet have duct tape covering her eyes as they pulled in.

"You're probably tired. You should lay down," the masked man commented before climbing out of the car. Exasperated, Connie wanted to respond. She wasn't tired. She just wanted to make sure Larry was okay. But she held back and lay down anyway.

"Put the duct tape and glasses back on."

She obeyed and heard the familiar sounds of a gas cap being unscrewed and gasoline being pumped. The strange thing was that this lasted for only a few seconds. Connie guessed that he couldn't have put in much more than a dollar's worth.

What was he doing? Was he checking to make sure they weren't followed?

A few minutes later and they were back on the road, headed back to the house where Connie hoped they would find Larry alive and unharmed. So far, her driver gave no indication that he suspected her of anything, or that anyone in his group was aware of the note she'd written or the conversation she'd had with Mark Hanson and Patty Hoogheem. Connie could only hope it would remain that way.

Mark Hanson waited only a few minutes after Patty locked the door before casually walking outside. It was not uncommon for him to take breaks during the day and walk to his truck for some fresh air. He went to his vehicle and acted as though he were getting something from it. Perhaps he could check the footage from the new security cameras soon. Perhaps they had picked up something helpful. But first he scanned the area for the kidnapper's car, for Connie, or for anything that might seem suspicious.

Nothing. It was time to alert the police. Mark dialed 911.[1]

CHAPTER SIX

WAITING GAME

Erie, Illinois

"We think your parents have been kidnapped."

The words silenced Jeff Van Oosten. Wyatt Heywaert was a longtime friend and also the Chief of Police in Albany, Illinois. He wouldn't call him up and joke about something like this.

"A bank teller at First Trust and Savings received a note from your mom while she was making a large withdrawal. We have a picture of the car we believe they've been taken in."

How do you respond when someone says something like this to you? The news sent Jeff into autopilot. He had just returned from the state of Washington earlier that afternoon. Tired from the cross-country flight, he had been looking forward to relaxing for the rest of the day. But now, all he could think about was what might be happening to his parents.

Someone kidnapped Mom and Dad? Why?

After quickly filling in his wife, Terri, he grabbed his keys and headed out the door. He had to go to his parents' house and get to the bottom of this if he could.

"Wait," Terri stopped him. "Don't you want your gun?" Jeff had a conceal and carry permit for the state of Illinois. Hardly believing what he was doing, he grabbed his gun and made the familiar drive to his mom and dad's.

The life of a busy family rarely slows down. Amy was at the school again, this time picking up her daughter after a team practice. Her phone rang, and she recognized Jeff's number.

"This has got to be a bad trick," he said, panic in his voice.

"What?"

"This has got to be a bad trick," Jeff said again. "Somebody just told me that Mom and Dad were kidnapped."

This seemed impossible to Amy. *Why would anyone do that?*

"That's ridiculous. I've got to pick up the kids. Just figure this out, and I'll call you back when I get home."

Jeff arrived at his parents' farmhouse. It was quiet—too quiet. He walked the path to the front door, a path he'd walked a thousand times before, but stopped abruptly before he entered.

Wait a minute. This is a crime scene.

He realized that he was the first one there. If anything he'd seen on TV shows and movies were true, then soon police officers were going to arrive and start investigating the premises. Still on autopilot and unable to process the reality of his parents being held against their will, Jeff turned around. He walked back to his truck and fell on his knees to pray. Since he was not typically one to make a big public display of his faith, this wouldn't have seemed normal to his family members. But on this day, nothing was normal. He prayed openly.

Jeff would later struggle to describe what happened next. "It was weird. It was like my brain shut off and I just had clarity."

The Erie Police and Whiteside County police were called to the scene. They arrived soon after Jeff had finished praying and began to question him. Though he didn't realize it at the time, it didn't look good that he was at the scene of a suspected crime. Family members are often at fault in cases like these.

The scene quickly became chaotic. Officers were going in and out. Yelling. Running. Shouting responses into their walkie talkies. Jeff watched from the driveway, dumbfounded, and trying to answer whatever question was posed to him.

"Do you know where your parents went last night?"

"Do you know what car they might be driving?"

"Did they have any vacation plans for this week?"

"Do you know if they were planning to travel out of town for any reason?"

The questions came at a bewildering pace. He never did go inside the house.

After a short while, the officers placed Jeff with Detective Bill Murray. The two stood together in the driveway and continued to watch the others in action, including the arrival of the S.W.A.T. team. The police organized their search efforts as the scene became less chaotic and more structured. The officers' training and rehearsed procedures became apparent. They started to move like a team.

It wasn't long before they found a broken window leading into the basement on the back side of the house. They found broken glass and drops of blood on the basement floor, as well as an unused taser in the lawn outside. They had clearly found the kidnapper's entrance. He or she must have received an injury during their entrance, presumably from the broken window. One of their first clues. There was also mud throughout the house, all over the carpet and flooring. There was more blood on the bed sheets and on the carpet around the bed.

Detective Murray continued to stick close to Jeff, asking more questions as they came up. The detective eventually offered the shell-shocked man a seat in his car. Jeff leaned his back against the car seat and tried to breathe normally. He couldn't believe what he was seeing. *Who would want to kidnap his mom and dad? Could this really be happening?* He had to call Amy again. He said a silent prayer and dialed her number.

The kidnapper's house

While the Van Oostens endured their captivity, the rest of the world continued on with a normal Tuesday in February. This included various friends and family members who expected to see them that day and throughout the week. It was imperative to their captor that the Van Oostens' disappearance go undiscovered in order for his plans to succeed. So, after returning from the bank, the man marched Connie straight to the same empty bedroom where he had forced her to make phone calls earlier. He needed her to make up a story to cover their disappearance—a lie that they had gone out of town together.

Connie tried to think. It was not at all like her and Larry to quickly leave town without telling anyone. If they were going to go on a trip, they would've made plans for weeks or even months in advance. Their kids, Jeff and Amy, and Larry's mom would've been among the first to know about their intentions. Not to mention their close friends and neighbors. What could she make up that would be believable?

"It's going to be hard to come up with something people will believe," Connie pointed out. The man moved the gun back and forth.

"Guess you better come up with something convincing. Just make them believe it." The man dropped a pad of paper and a pencil on the floor.

What was he thinking? After no food or sleep . . . and after having to come up with a plan to get the check from the bank . . . after all that had happened, how could he possibly think she was capable of coming up with some fairytale about why they were gone? Tears formed in her eyes. She was frightened and angry. If he were going to kill them, then it had to end soon.

"Write down a story as to why you're out of town. I want to look at it."

Connie had spent years traveling and talking with people of all kinds. Her plainspoken honesty had paid off with her customers. Would it pay off with this man?

"They're not going to believe me," she remarked plainly. "We don't just leave town."

"I don't care. Just convince them."

With tears in her eyes, Connie began to write. She tried to think of something, anything that might seem plausible. They had a week full of plans to see their friends and family. What could she say that wouldn't sound like a lie?

Just as he was leaving the room, he turned to Connie.

"I have a daughter," he said after a few minutes. Connie's ears perked up. He was actually talking about himself.

"I was in Special Ops. In the military. I worked for some *horrible* people. The people I work for now . . . , they're horrible people, too."

"Can't you leave? Can't you find something else to do?"

"No. If I don't follow through with this, they will hurt me and my daughter."

Connie remained quiet for a minute. What else could she say to somehow change this situation?

Iowa

Amy was still incredulous as she returned home and ushered the kids inside. *Kidnapped*? It seemed too bizarre to be true. Who would want to kidnap her mom and dad? Still, she went outside when she saw her brother calling again. She wanted to talk privately.

"Seriously, get in the car. You've got to come over here," Jeff blurted, still panicked.

Not willing to throw her young family into a panic until she had more information, Amy quickly thought of a cover story for her kids and husband, John. Three days a week she worked in the office at Quality Interiors in Erie. The 45-minute drive from her home in Iowa would have to be made again, but it would also give her time to talk with Jeff in more depth.

"I need to get out to the store and pick something up," she said to her kids. "Dad will be home in ten minutes." Amy called her husband, John, and told him the same story before climbing into her car.

On the road, Amy called Jeff back. On the drive across the state line, Amy heard everything he knew up to that point—the house swarming with officers, the S.W.A.T. team, the conversations with Detective Murray, and the video.

"I guess mom was on camera at the bank," he said. "She didn't look normal. And no one has heard from them. The people at the bank thought something was wrong. She was trying to withdraw all their money."

"When was the last time you talked with Dad?" Amy asked Jeff, knowing that he called Larry almost every day.

"I don't know. When was the last time you talked with Mom?"

As Jeff does with Larry, Amy calls Connie nearly every day, too.

For the next several minutes the siblings tried to figure out how long it had been since either of them had heard from their parents. It dawned on both of them that neither really had a clue as to their whereabouts.

Jeff had called Larry numerous times earlier in the day. He had been agitated that Larry hadn't called him back yet—unusual behavior for his dad. Now the reason was becoming clear.

The drive from Iowa to Erie, Illinois, would be considered quiet and scenic by most travelers. Interstate 80 runs east, skirting across the north side of the town of Davenport, Iowa, before dipping south toward the bridge, crossing the Mississippi River at the small town of Rapids City, Illinois. Across the state line the route takes a diagonal turn to the northeast, across farmland on I-88 toward Erie. It's a drive dotted with proud homes, hard-working farms, and open country.

Amy's thoughts were not on the scenery as she sped to Erie. Worry and anxiety rode along with her.

As Amy made this trip, law enforcement officers officially declared Connie and Larry Van Oostens' house a crime scene. They began the next phase of the investigation by combing through their home. Their office. Their computers. Their financial records. They examined anything they could find that might give them a clue as to the couple's whereabouts.

Jeff, meanwhile, was still being kept at the end of the driveway by the police as he talked on and off with Amy.

"We can't have you accidentally contaminating the crime scene," they said. Though he didn't yet realize it, he was still their prime suspect. What better place to keep him than surrounded by officers at the scene?

As Amy neared Erie, Illinois, she received another call. It was the Erie Police Department. They ask her to meet them at the Erie exit, just off Interstate 88.

"We need your keys to your parents' store," they said.

Do they think someone is hiding them at the store? Amy wondered. *Or do they need to get money out of the store?*

A large grain bin sits at the Erie exit. Amy met two police cars near the structure.

"I can unlock the store for you."

"No. It's too dangerous," one of them said seriously. "You cannot go to the store. And you cannot go to your parents' house. There are police everywhere."

Without further explanation, Amy handed over her keys. The officers left, leaving her to guess at what was happening with her parents.

This is totally surreal, Amy thought. *I just can't believe what I'm hearing.*

Without anywhere else to go in Erie, Amy went to Jeff's house. Terri and their three children were home, along with Terri's mom, who was trying to keep the kids occupied in the basement. Jeff's best friend, Jason, and his wife, Amy, as well as their minister, Terry Green, had heard the news and were there for support.

They sat together, unsure of what to say or do. As they waited, Amy called and texted Jeff multiple times, hoping he might have information on the police investigation because he was actually at their parents' home, and because of his friendship with Chief Heywaert. But no new information came from the chief.[2]

The kidnapper's house

The house was quiet. Larry was alone and waiting for his wife to return. They could be in a house in a wide-open field, like a buoy on Lake Michigan, just a dot on the horizon. They might be separated by miles from the nearest neighbor. Or they could be nestled on a normal street at the end of a cul-de-sac, surrounded by other homes full of bustling families. A prison obscured by white picket fences. He had no idea one way or another. He just knew that he and Connie had only each other and the God of their prayers.

"We know that in all things God works for the good of those who love him." Larry repeated the verse to himself and prayed.

It was approaching 7:00 p.m. and already dark outside, typical for Illinois in February. It was cold and dark outside, but this was nothing compared to the darkness and evil that held the Van Oostens captive.

After returning from the bank, the masked man marched Connie into the empty spare bedroom. She heard Larry's phone ring. After quickly examining the number, the man clicked the button, forcing the call to voicemail. Connie couldn't see or hear anyone else in the house.

Was the rest of the group still at the bank? Was Larry still down in the room? Was he okay? She could only hope the check their captor had obtained was all that he wanted. *Isn't $350,000 enough?*

"We're going to make some calls about your investments," he said flatly.

How did this man know about their savings? How did he know about their investments and whom to call? And how could he have had all the papers ready for them to sign back the house? How big was this group, and what else did they know?

With her eyes always averted from looking at her captor, and always with the gun visible within her peripheral vision, Connie began to make more phone calls as demanded of her.

Larry's phone rang again. Agitated by the interruption, the man clicked it off. "That was Jeff."

The phone rang again. The man clicked it off again, this time more forcefully.

"I keep getting this phone call from Jeff. He's been calling all day."

"That's because he talks to his dad every day," Connie said. The phone rang again.

"Won't he stop?" he asked.

"No." Were the circumstances different, Connie might have smiled. If there was one thing about her son she knew beyond the shadow of doubt, it was that he wouldn't give up on reaching his dad. He was stubborn that way.

"He's not going to quit." She may as well have been announcing that flames burn and water is wet. Some things are just a matter of fact. "He's just going to keep calling. He will *not quit*."

The man considered his options. The phone rang again in his hand, and he clicked it off.

"That's not going to work."

"What will it take to make him stop, then?"

"Let me talk to him."

"You had *better* be convincing."

The masked man reluctantly allowed Connie to take Jeff's next call. Anything to make him stop calling, further slowing down his plans. He held the gun closer to her, taking up more of her peripheral vision as a reminder of what would happen should she say or do anything suspicious while she spoke with her son.

"Hi, Jeff." Connie began telling him a longer version of the story she'd told Amy the previous day. "We just went out of town for a few days. We'll be back soon."

"Where'd you go?" Jeff asked.

"We went up to Schaumburg."

"Where are you?" Jeff asked.

"We're at a gas station."

"Let me talk to Dad." Connie thought of Larry, still handcuffed in the basement.

"He can't talk. He's paying for the gas."

As the conversation continued, Connie could feel the man growing more and more agitated. The way he moved about the room, clearly uncomfortable with all of this time spent with Connie talking on the phone. Jeff's characteristic persistence wasn't helping. Throughout their call, he seemed to ask the same questions multiple times.

"Where are you? And where's Dad?" Every lie, every evasion of Jeff's questions, was a challenge. It was hard to hide the stress from her voice. It was hard to weave a lie for her son that rang with any amount of truth. But she had to appease Jeff and get him off the phone, not just for her safety and Larry's, but for his as well. Even if he didn't know it.

"Well, I'm out at the farm," Jeff finally said. "And I can't find the air compressor. Would you ask Dad where it is?"

Fear gripped her heart again. The kidnapper had said he planned to return to the farm to pick up some things. Would he find Jeff there? What would happen to her son?

I will ask your dad—just hang on," Connie said. The man grabbed the phone from the floor, muted the microphone, and stomped from the room. Connie remained in her spot on the bedroom floor, knowing that someone else in the group was probably watching her on video. She thought about the note she'd written and all that had happened at the bank. *God, please send us help soon.*

Using the speaker system, the man spoke to Larry. It was the first time he had spoken to him since their arrival at this house.

"Where do you keep your air compressor?" he asked, using his voice modulator.

"What?"

"Where is the air compressor at your farm? Your son wants to know where it is."

This is totally strange, Larry thought. *Jeff knows right where it is.* So, Larry purposely told him the wrong location in the hope of letting Jeff know something was wrong.

"I had no idea what was going on," Larry would say later. "I just had to do what was expected."

The man told Connie the answer and put the phone back on the floor. It was time to end this call. Fortunately, Jeff seemed to finally relent with his questions.

"We'll be home in just a few days," she said as their call ended. "I love you."

Jeff hung up his phone and took a steadying breath. He looked at Detective Murray and the group of agents standing around him at his parents' farm. Hopefully he'd done his job well and kept his mom talking long enough. He wished he could've heard his dad's voice, too, just to be sure he was okay.

"Did you get it?" Murray asked an FBI agent. A moment's pause.

"We got it. They're somewhere in Geneseo."

The FBI had spoken with Larry's cellular phone service provider. They were using Jeff's conversation to trace the call to a specific location. Geneseo wasn't far. Another small town in farm country. At least they had a start.

The kidnapper realized it was too late in the evening to make another call to the bank, but there were still additional monies he wanted released. After a few minutes of silent thinking, he made a startling confession.

"It's my job to keep you for two weeks; then I will have to kill you." Connie waited in silence, staring at the carpet on the empty floor of the bedroom. "But if you do everything I say, then I won't hurt your family."

As Connie sat in silence, letting this information sink in, the kidnapper pushed forward with his plans. He decided to force Larry to record a phone message authorizing the release of the money. He did this by sending Connie back down the ladder and handing her a recording device through the door in the floor. She held it up for Larry, and he recorded the message. There was something about the message he didn't like, so he had Connie record a new one. She handed it back up to him.

While knowing that Larry was okay brought Connie some measure of relief, their captor was at the same time clearly growing restless—waving his gun, pacing the room, and making sharper demands. The cold, mechanical veneer was starting to crack. He was unhappy with how long it was taking to get the money secured, and he still seemed to be upset about the frustrating calls with the bank in Erie from earlier that day. The question was, what would his unhappiness mean?

Albany, Illinois
First Trust and Savings Bank

The hours following Mark Hanson's 911 call were a flurry of activity at the bank.

"That's when things got crazy," Hanson would say later. "I told the police we had a hostage situation. That we'd given Connie a check that would be impossible to cash, and that we had limited time to help."

Officers responded immediately, arriving at the bank to interview Mark and other staff members. After learning of the seriousness of the situation, the local police called the FBI. Mark, Patty, other bank staff members, and law enforcement agents would be at the bank until past midnight, investigating the crime.

The newly installed security cameras paid off. "We had a great visual of the car—an old, silver Chevy Caprice—but we couldn't make out the license plate numbers." Mark told the officers. "We can actually see her get into the car and the car drive off."

Security cameras also had plenty of footage of Connie entering the bank and in conversation with Patty and Mark.

During the evening hours of Wednesday, February 8, FBI and other law enforcement worked with Hanson and bank staff to investigate the company the check was made out to, Store Edge LLC. Every business in the state of Illinois has to be registered through the Illinois Secretary of State's office. One of the police detectives working the case had done undercover work that had involved similar circumstances. Following his directions, they looked through the Secretary of State records for Store Edge LLC.

At the same time, they searched the Secretary of State records for the registration of the Chevrolet Caprice that had been seen on video. They found a match—sort of.

Store Edge LLC and the Caprice were registered to the same name, though it was spelled differently. The two were not a perfect match. Whether the name had been misspelled by accident or to obscure the man's identity, the police and FBI couldn't be sure. Regardless, the detectives wrote down the name for further investigation. Perhaps they were on to something.

"Either they'll try to cash it," Mark told the officers that night, "or they'll deposit it into an account they already have set up." Since the LLC wasn't registered, this would indicate that the kidnappers would have to have someone working with them on the inside of a bank to set up this account.

"We might get a call from another bank to see whether the check is good," Mark told the FBI.

"Tell them it's *not*," was their firm response.

"But if we let them try to cash it, we might get fingerprints and video."

Mark's reasoning was sound, but, ultimately, the FBI's decision to avoid cashing the check stood. The kidnappers would not be receiving the money they'd planned on getting.

Around 9:00 p.m. on Wednesday night, Jeff returned to his home. By that time his parents' close friends, Vernon and Lonavene, as well as their pastor, Terry Green, had come over to wait with the family at Jeff's house. He began to fill everyone in as best he could, careful not to scare his children, though unable to keep them from knowing what was going on.

The tension in the home was palpable. No one knew what to do but wait and pray for their safety. Unanswered questions filled the room like the fog that had recently blanketed Erie. All they could do was stare at each other, pace the room, and pray.

A break in the tension came in the form of a call from the FBI. "We need you and Amy to come to the bank in Albany." The FBI wanted to talk with both them, offering to share what they knew of their parents' disappearance.

Vernon drove the pair of worried siblings because he didn't want them to drive in their anxious state.

"They say they have Mom on camera," Jeff said again. "And that she didn't look normal."

Didn't look normal. They could only guess at what that meant and hope that the police would have answers for them.

But at the bank they were greeted by FBI agents. "We have a few questions we'd like to ask each of you, separately."

Jeff and Amy were quickly separated into different rooms, where they discovered that they were suspects in their parents' disappearance. It was time for their interrogations to begin.

Meanwhile, the senior Van Oostens were together in the underground room. Larry was unharmed, and Connie had seen no signs of the other kidnappers. With cameras watching them and a microphone listening, there was little they could say or do without risk. Anything they discussed would be overheard and analyzed. Anything they might do would be seen. They couldn't talk of escape or attempt to open the door to the main floor. Not only their lives, but the lives of children and grandchildren were at stake.

Connie couldn't even tell Larry about all that had transpired at the bank. If she told him about her note, or about her conversations with Mark and Patty, then who knew how the kidnappers would react? Surely it would mean their deaths.

They settled in for the night. Low on the floor, in the sparse, small room they just waited. Neither could sleep again.

Why are they not coming for us? Connie wondered. *Wasn't my note enough to make something happen? Why are they not here? Why is this taking so long?*

FBI agents led Jeff into one office and Amy into another for their interrogations. Each sat with two FBI agents. Amy's interrogation was comprised mostly of questions about the business.

"Who knows how much money your parents might have?"

"Who do they have investments with?"

"Who has recently contacted them with a business proposition?"

"What do you know about their finances?"

"Is anyone threatening them?"

"Would anyone have reason to steal from them?"

"Would anyone want to hurt them?"

Amy couldn't imagine who would want to hurt her parents. The answer to almost every question was "no."

"Everybody loves them," she told the agents. "They are Sunday school teachers. They are very involved in their church."

Then they asked, "Do you know if anyone has been in their house recently?"

The answer came to mind immediately. Though Amy didn't want to say his name for fear that he might be considered a suspect, she answered the question. "He works for us. He's our carpet installer."

The agents wrote down his name.

"People judge a book by its cover when they see him," Amy said, thinking of his tattoos and piercings. "But he's one of the kindest men. He's a great employee."

Though she gave the FBI his name, Amy couldn't believe it was him.

"He's been nothing but fabulous to our family and our family business," she said.

Jeff's interrogation was much less pleasant than Amy's. He would learn that night that the FBI has little time to be kind or compassionate. They must act quickly to get the information they need if they have any hope of finding victims alive. Also, they must be thorough in their investigation. If they are not, the case could get derailed in the court of law.

In most cases of a kidnapping, the prime suspects are first those who were kidnapped—assuming they'd faked a disappearance—and then those closest to them.

"What are your finances?"

"I'm thirty years old. I've got three kids and a house. I'm kind of in the middle of them right now," Jeff said. "They're not great, but they're not terrible."

"If you had a problem, what would you do?"

On and on the probing questions came, increasingly making Jeff feel lost and angry. *How and why would they think he could have anything to do with something like this? Why am I getting lumped into this?*

"Would you go to your parents if you were in financial trouble?"

Jeff paused for a minute. The stubborn streak he'd inherited from Larry was alive and well inside him. "Well, the last thing I would want to do is ask my parents for help. But if they wanted to help me, and if I really needed it, they would probably just give me the money."

After a long hour of questioning that made him feel unjustly suspected, the agents seemed satisfied. He knew they were just doing their job, and yet he couldn't believe that they would even think it was him. All he wanted to do was find his parents.

After an hour of interrogation, Amy and Jeff were allowed to get back together. The FBI led them to chairs in the lobby of the bank. It was then that the branch manager, Mark Hanson, came over and hugged them both.

"I'm so sorry. I'm so sorry I couldn't stop them," Hanson said to the weary siblings. "I just want you to know that I'm opening this bank for everything. Anything I can do to help, I will."

The agents told Amy and Jeff a little bit about what was happening, but not every detail of the investigation. They were told that Connie had come in at closing time and that a teller had gotten the note from her, claiming that she was being held at gunpoint. They knew the teller took it right to Mark and that he had done all he could to keep their mother safe.

Amy and Jeff were also shown the surveillance footage of their mother. She did indeed look unwell.

"She never leaves the house without doing her hair and at least a little bit of makeup," Amy observed. "She's not put together at all like she normally would be." This only confirmed the FBI's suspicions.

The two stayed at the bank until after 11:00 p.m. before they were cleared to leave. It had been only a little over six hours since Jeff had first told Amy that their parents were missing, yet each hour had taken double its normal toll.

A police officer on the scene took the siblings to Morrison, Illinois, a small town 15 miles east of Albany, to the Whiteside

County Sheriff's Department, home of the county jail. Here they would sit and wait in another lobby, but what they saw there amazed them.

A massive number of officers, teams, and precincts were reporting for duty to find the Van Oostens that night. There were so many officers from so many different locations around Erie that Jeff and Amy quickly lost count. They couldn't believe so many people would be looking for their parents.

"It *blew my mind* to see how well they all worked together. It was seamless," Jeff would report later.

"It really was astounding," Amy confirmed. "We probably weren't supposed to be listening in, but we couldn't help but overhear the officers as they checked in. There were officers from *all over*. It was amazing."

Sixteen agencies took part in the investigation. Among those on the case included the FBI; the Illinois State Police; police departments from Erie, Albany, Fulton, Rock Falls, Prophetstown, Morrison, Whiteside County,[3] Lee County, Dixon, Geneseo; the Rock Island County Sheriff's department; the Henry County Sheriff's department; and the Quad City Airport Police.[4]

As the two of them sat and listened, they began to discuss calling their extended family. Should we call Dad's brother and sister? Should we call Mom's sisters and brother?

"We probably should, but I can't do it," Jeff admitted, the hours, the interrogation, and the anxiety having taken their toll.

Amy began to make some calls.

One of her first was to Larry's sister and her daughter. She'd been in contact with them that evening already. They were keeping an eye on Grandma, Larry's mother. The 89-year-old was not yet aware of all that was transpiring. She typically went to bed around 7:00 or 8:00 p.m. Amy asked her aunt to go over there and keep Grandma from watching the evening news. They would decide the next day what they would tell her. They didn't want to upset her if they didn't have to. Amy called to give her aunt what little update she had.

Amy also called Larry's brother in Florida, as well as one of her mom's sisters, asking her to contact the rest of Connie's family.

"Please keep it to yourselves until we know more," she told them. "The police are working so hard on it."

For the first time during that long, horrible night, the Van Oosten siblings had hope. If this many officers and agencies were on the case, then surely they'd be able to find their parents. *Right?*

After midnight
Cambridge, Illinois

FBI agents arrived at another home in Cambridge, this one belonging to the Van Oostens' carpet installer. After being allowed entry, they asked him to step outside and interrogated him in the street. The bewildered man obeyed immediately. As with Jeff's interrogation, there was no doubt about why they were asking questions. He was another suspect in the kidnapping of Larry and Connie Van Oosten.

"I was interrogated too," Mark Hanson would say later. "They thought *I* was a suspect. They say they're just doing their job, but it puts a weird feeling in your stomach when you're helping somebody and then you get interrogated."

Thorough police work is unbiased and unforgiving. It would take thorough police work to find Larry and Connie, no matter how unpleasant it might be.

Erie, Illinois
Jeff Van Oosten's house

At nearly 1:00 a.m. on Thursday, February 9, a police officer brought Amy and Jeff back to Jeff's house. His kids were still awake, and all three were frightened. "What's going to happen to Grandma and Grandpa?" was a question he didn't have an answer for.

Amy had stayed in touch with her husband, John, throughout the night. Their fourteen-year-old daughter knew something was wrong, while their nine-year-old son was asleep. She told John to be brief and vague when explaining the night's events to their children. "We can't find Grandma and Grandpa, but we're working on it."

John was up with his daughter for most of the night. She fell asleep that night in her parents' bed, crying and scared for her grandma and grandpa.

She's my worrier, Amy thought.

Feeling exhausted, Amy lay on the couch. Her two nieces kept close to her, virtually lying on top of her, both scared for their grandparents. They found themselves in the same place they'd been hours before: just sitting together in Jeff's house, wide awake, worried, unable to do anything to help, and filled with questions.

As before, the tension was broken when Jeff's phone rang.

"It was the police. They need me to come in," he said.

"Do they know something?" asked Amy.

"No, they just want me to come back to the sheriff's office."

Something didn't feel right to Amy. "Well, it's 1:00 o'clock in the morning. We don't know where Mom and Dad are. We don't know who has them."

"I don't know. They said they're just sending a car for me."

"How do you know it's actually police?" Amy asked, worry creeping into her voice. She recalled what they had learned at the bank, that her mother was concerned that their captor might be part of a larger group. That there was likely a team of people involved. "How do you know it's not . . . how do you *know* that somebody's not coming *for you*?"

"I have to trust," Jeff replied. "They said they have more questions for me."

There was no end in sight for the nightmare they were enduring. Amy began to cry.

Why not me? Why don't I get to go? Why don't I get to know more?

The vehicle that arrived to take Jeff was an unmarked car.

What if my brother is currently being kidnapped?

Amy watched him walk out, wondering whether he was being kidnapped in front of her eyes.

Did I just let him go, too?

Police department headquarters

After experiencing one interrogation, Jeff knew to expect that this visit might not be all that friendly.

"Look, you can ask whatever you want," he said quickly. "I just want to make sure my parents get found. I really don't care what you ask me. Just do what you have to do."

Question after question followed. These were even more in depth than those that had been asked earlier at the bank. The detectives wanted information about Jeff's personal finances, his parents' business, and more details about his relationship with them. Interrogations are not concerned with privacy or manners. They are about ascertaining facts that might lead to the truth.

In another situation, Jeff might've gotten really angry with someone asking him about these things. Yet even in a plain cinderblock room without windows, feeling the strain of a long day and looking at two detectives, Jeff experienced a calmness he could not explain.

"We'd like you to tell us about someone." The detectives mentioned the name of someone in Erie, someone Jeff had known for years but whom he hadn't spent any time with in . . . he couldn't remember how long. The detectives seemed to be directing their questioning around this man. His was the name connected to both Store Edge LLC and the Chevrolet Caprice.

"Nah, it wouldn't be him," Jeff said. "We haven't had anything to do with him, or even really talked to him, in years." The detectives continued to push.

"He was valedictorian. A year ahead of me in school. Everybody talked about how smart he is. He was in youth group and knew the Bible inside and out. He always had all the right answers. It wouldn't be him. There's no way."

Their questioning moved on to other topics. To Jeff's relief, the detectives eventually came to the conclusion that if Jeff had really needed some money, he could just have gone to his parents and asked for it.

Then, suddenly, there was commotion in the hallway. People were running, visible as passing blurs in a small window in the metal door.

What in the world? Jeff wondered.

The detectives escorted him to the waiting area and left quickly. There seemed to be total chaos as he waited and watched. People were running everywhere. Detective Bill Murry found him.

"Come on. I'm your ride home."

Inside the car there was more commotion on the detective's radio, but Murray seemed to be keeping it low.

What is going on?

CHAPTER SEVEN

HIGH-SPEED CHASE

Thursday, February 9, 2017
Villages of Erie and Port Byron, Illinois

The kidnapper drove his silver Chevy Caprice to the Van Oostens' home. He wanted to clean up the broken glass in the basement. It was late, well into the early morning hours. The Van Oostens were locked in for the night, probably lying awake, scared under the gaze of his cameras. He had the check for $350,000. No one had followed them from the bank. With any luck, he would get his hands on their investments the next day. Everything was going according to plan.

But everything was not really going as he would've hoped, though there was no way he could have known. He couldn't have known of the investigation that had been underway for the last number of hours at the bank. He didn't know that images of his car had been recorded by the security cameras at the bank in Albany, and that all officers and agents from 16 agencies were on high alert for just such a car. He had no idea that, after hours of work, one officer who was experienced with this type of scheme from another case had been able to track down who the check was really meant for . . . and the real name behind the fake corporation printed on the check.

Officers from the Erie Police Department had been posted round the clock at the Van Oosten home. Two officers guarded the perimeter. The man drove down their road and toward their driveway. Seeing a squad car parked by the house, he did not pull in but passed casually by. One officer standing vigil that night saw the aging Caprice, asked incredulously, "Isn't that the car we're looking for?" and put his own car into gear immediately.

With his lights flashing, the officer indicated for the masked man to pull over just down the road from the Van Oosten residence. However, as the officer approached the masked man's window, he stepped on the gas. A high-speed chase was underway!

Through the back roads of Illinois farm country, the masked man raced his old car. Would the deep darkness of February help him evade the law, as it had once helped him sneak across a muddy field?

The chase traveled west, out of Erie and toward the river and the state line. Radios sounded from one officer's car to the next. More squad cars joined the chase. Police radios came to life as the chase continued.

"In pursuit of suspect driving a silver Chevrolet Caprice. Suspect is heading west . . . "

The chase stretched to Port Byron, Illinois, a small village along the Mississippi River about 14 miles from Erie. They touched speeds of eighty miles per hour as they sped down roads with farmland on either side. Neighboring homes were quiet and dark in the early morning hours.

The masked man eventually lost control of his vehicle. He hit another car that was traveling in the opposite direction—a head-on collision that quickly ended his escape.

As officers approached and pulled him from the car, his first words were, "How did you know it was me?"

The officers on the scene quickly identified their prime suspect in the abduction of Larry and Connie Van Oosten. A man identified through the FBI's investigation that had begun at First Trust and Savings Bank. One Chad C. Schipper of Geneseo, Illinois, was arrested and taken into police custody.

The driver of the other car was transported to the hospital with no severe injuries. Upon inspection, of the Caprice officers found a wig and a handgun.

The next day, the *Quad-City Times* posted an article with the following headline:

ARREST MADE IN REPORTED WHITESIDE COUNTY ABDUCTION

Deputies located a vehicle that the suspect, Chad C. Schipper, 40, was driving. Schipper fled authorities and a high-speed chase ensued.

Schipper, of rural Geneseo, was arrested and was taken to a local hospital to be treated for non-life-threatening injuries he suffered in the crash.[5]

During the ride in the ambulance, Schipper spoke to officer Wyatt Heywaert about the officer's father, Tim, whom Schipper knew. After all he had done, Schipper tried to speak as though he and Heywaert were old friends.

Not having any of it, the officer told Schipper, "You need to stop talking."

Finally, the masked man was unmasked.

CHAPTER EIGHT

FREEDOM

Erie, Illinois

Hours passed. It was almost 4:30 a.m. on Thursday morning, February 9. Larry and Connie Van Oosten had been held captive for nearly a full 48 hours. Amy was still awake and talking with her sister-in-law, unaware of any high-speed chase happening nearby.

"Should I head over to Grandma's?" Amy asked.

"This early? Why?"

"She wakes up this early." Her grandmother had gone to bed early on Wednesday, before any news of the abduction was released on the local news broadcast. Amy imagined her grandmother turning on the morning news and hearing for the first time about her son and daughter-in-law's plight.

How would an elderly woman handle that? What questions would she have? Could her heart handle the shock?

"I've got to go," Amy decided, grabbing her purse. "If you hear from Jeff, tell him I went to Grandma's house."

Amy made the short drive across Erie to her grandmother's home. The streets were mostly empty in the early morning darkness. For all the light the streetlamps made, they also seemed to create pockets of impenetrable shadows. *Were her parents hidden in some similar shadow? Were they even in Erie?*

Amy pulled into the driveway but decided to wait in the car and call her grandmother first. That seemed like a better idea than just appearing at the door.

"It's me, Grandma. I'm okay, but can I please come in?"

Her grandmother seemed shaken when she opened the door.

"Amy," she said with an uncertain smile. "What are you doing here so early?"

As much as she didn't want to, Amy told her 89-year-old grandmother the grim news, watching the shock and confusion cloud her face. All they could do was hug one another, pray, and wait.

Port Byron, the scene of the collision

"I didn't hurt them," Chad Schipper said to the officers questioning him. "I took good care of them. It wasn't that big of a deal." No matter what he said, the deputy on the scene did not believe him.

"Where are they?"

"They're at a house in Geneseo." Schipper gave them the address. A call was immediately placed to the FBI, who were already outside the home. Schipper owned multiple properties across three counties. The FBI had officers at all of them, which had been a significant effort to coordinate. As soon as they had probable cause, they could enter the properties and conduct a search for Larry and Connie. Statistically speaking, they did not expect to find the Van Oostens alive.

"It really wasn't a big deal," Schipper repeated. But try as he might to play down his actions, the FBI had everything they needed. It was time to move in.

Geneseo, Illinois, in the kidnapper's house, a property owned by Chad Schipper

It was between 4:00 and 5:00 a.m. when Larry and Connie heard footsteps above them.

"I think this is it," Larry whispered gravely. "Are you ready? This is probably the end."

For two days and two nights the Van Oostens had been treated as though their lives didn't matter in the least. Almost everything had been taken from them. Their freedom. Their home. Communication with their loved ones. Their savings. Their health and wellbeing. Their privacy and dignities. Nothing was sacred to the group that was holding them captive. Every violent action was done as though it were no big deal. They'd spent their lives around farmers who'd taken better care of and shown more human decency to their animals than they had received from their masked captor.

Neither was certain they would make it out of that house alive. Though they'd prayed continuously to God for safety and deliverance, they understood that God doesn't always answer prayers the way people think he should—but does answer in a way that is best for them. They had, however, quietly discussed a plan to leave Larry's handcuffs unlocked the next time Connie was instructed to cuff him to the wall. If the man came down again, Larry would be ready. Yet they had no concrete plans of escape. Their main concern was to do what they were told in order to protect their kids and grandkids, even if that meant forfeiting their own lives.

"Are you ready?" Larry whispered again. "We should pray one more time. They got the money and probably realized they can't get any more."

The noise upstairs continued. In fact, it seemed to be getting louder. There were multiple people walking everywhere. The team the man had told them about must be above them. This was how they would die. Killed by professional criminals who had done this to countless others, . . . and would do so again.

Sitting on the edge of the mattress, overwhelmed by stress and exhaustion, Larry asked God to deliver them—and, even if he didn't, to watch over their loved ones. Almost instantly a fresh sense of peace covered them. It was indescribable. Like nothing they'd felt before this experience. They were not out of danger. In fact, they were fairly sure they were not going to make it home alive. But whatever happened next, they weren't concerned about it in the same way. God would be with them. No matter what.

But the commotion upstairs continued. The sound of footsteps by multiple people was unmistakable. They sounded as though they were right above them, then as though they had walked away. Were they getting ready to kill them? Were they unloading their surveillance equipment from the house? The lock on the steel-plated door was being moved. This was it. Their final moments. Someone kept working with the lock. It almost sounded as though they couldn't get it open. They were starting to yell. Then Larry and Connie heard the sound of bolt cutters.

"Who's there?" they both yelled into the dark. "Who's there?!"

"It's the FBI! We're here for you!"

The next thing they knew the door was pulled open and a young FBI agent jumped into the room without waiting for the ladder. He immediately checked the room for threats. Once he was certain they weren't in danger, he pulled them into a hug.

"They're okay! They're okay!" he shouted up to the main floor. Connie and Larry were speechless. *Was this really happening?*

"We've been looking for you." He smiled. Everything had changed in an instant.

The next several minutes were a blur of rejoicing, of activity, and of questions. *Was it over? Was it really over?*

The Van Oostens were brought upstairs, where they met a team of six FBI agents, as well as police detectives. The house was filled and surrounded by law enforcement officials.

Only moments before they had expected to meet a team of masked criminals. They'd expected to find kidnappers and thieves who were ready to dispose of them. But, instead, they were meeting a team of agents and officers, each one armed and ready to defend them with their lives. The turnabout was so extreme that it was hard to process it all. Their prayers had been answered.

They were seated on the hearth of a fireplace in the living room and gently asked the first of many questions that would follow over the next several days. After a few minutes, Connie saw out of the corner of her eye that she was sitting right next to a pair of assault rifles carried by the agents, but that had been set on the floor, as they did their work.

"I'm sorry, ma'am," one agent said, noticing her glances at the weapons. "Are those bothering you?"

Connie smiled. "No. I'm kind of glad you have them." The agent nodded kindly, understanding as best he could. For once, the gun wasn't pointed at her but was there for her protection.

Someone called an ambulance for them. After two days of captivity in a secret room of an average home on an average street in the small town of Geneseo, Illinois, Larry and Connie Van Oosten were free.

CHAPTER NINE

REVELATIONS

Shortly after 5:00 a.m., Erie, Illinois

"Where are you?" Jeff Van Oosten yelled into his phone. "I have news!"

Minutes later Jeff arrived at his grandmother's house and pounded on the front door, startling both Amy and his grandmother.

"They found them! They found them!" The next few minutes were as joyful as any he had experienced before. The three stood in the living room and hugged for a long time, crying tears of joy and praying "Thank you," over and over. It was a sacred moment. Their family had been pulled apart by evil, but evil had not won the day.

When the moment passed, Jeff and Amy decided to stay with their grandmother. Eventually Larry's sister and her daughter came over. The family waited for more updates from the police.

At some point amid the chaos Amy asked Jeff, "Where have you been? You were gone from like 2:00 to 4:00 in the morning. What do you know?"

"I was at the police department. I wanted to call you really bad, but they said it was too time sensitive. That they didn't want me making any phone calls."

Around 10:00 a.m. they finally got the call they'd been waiting for. Hammond Henry Hospital in Geneseo called Jeff. It was time for a joyful reunion.

Amy and Jeff were the only two members of the family to head to the hospital. The rest would need to wait for the time being. They rode from Erie to Geneseo, passing farmland that only hours before had been the place their parents were held captive.

"Do you know how they're doing? Are they injured? Are they okay?" Amy asked.

Jeff didn't know. The FBI agent who had invited them to the hospital had not given him that information.

"Did he say who will be there?" Amy asked. Jeff shook his head.

What were they going to find at the hospital exactly? Amy wondered. *The police? FBI? . . . The kidnappers?*

"Amy," Jeff said, interrupting her thoughts, "I know *who* it was." During his last call with the police, one of the officers had told Jeff who was in custody.

"What?! What do you mean?"

"You're never . . . you're *never* going believe who it is."

"I *know* them?"

"Yeah. It was Chad Schipper."

How? How could it possibly be him? The questions popped in Amy's mind, but no answers come. She knew Chad Schipper.

In fact, she'd known him for years. They'd grown up in Erie. Everyone pretty much knew everyone else. They attended the same church and school. In high school Chad was soft-spoken and smart. He eventually became the valedictorian of his class. He wasn't anyone she thought would someday be capable of a crime. None of this made any sense.

"Something I said must've clicked with the cops," Jeff said. "I mentioned his name last night when they interrogated me again. They were asking me about their finances. I told them that a while back Chad had tried to sell them investments, and then they started asking a lot questions about him."

Connie and Larry had told Amy about meeting Chad years ago about an investment opportunity. It was a drop in an everyday bucket of conversation. She vaguely remembered her parents saying, "Oh yeah, Chad Schipper is trying to get into being a financial advisor. We're going to talk to him just cause we've known him for forever, but nothing will probably come of it."

It was completely unbelievable that any of this could have stemmed from that conversation.

Amy and Jeff arrived at Hammond Henry Hospital and entered through the Emergency Room doors. The first people they met were some of the same FBI agents who had interrogated them at the bank.

"They're okay! They're just getting checked out." After two interrogations, Jeff was glad that for this meeting he was not sitting again on the opposite side of a table from agents.

Larry and Connie had been put in separate rooms, each sitting for an interview with the FBI and State Police. The officers and agents were considerate and compassionate. After all they'd been through, it was a relief to be with people who cared.

Larry was ready for checkout first. When the officers opened his room door, Jeff and Amy rushed inside to see their dad. They had never been so happy to see him.

After a few minutes of tearful hellos, Larry learned the identity of their captor. Suddenly everything started to come together. The memories of the last 72 hours swam through his mind on a current he couldn't keep up with. Suddenly everything made sense. "He saw all my investments. He knew what we had." But *why*? There were still plenty of questions that needed answering, but they would have to wait.

After a few minutes the officers opened the doors to Connie's room across the hall.

"It was the best sight I've ever saw in my life," Amy would say later.

Amid all the hugs and prayers and tears of joy, Amy could sense that her mom was a different person when she came out of the hospital room. Connie latched on and just kept hugging her.

The following minutes were a mix of head-spinning and heartwarming. Doctors. Nurses. Police officers. FBI agents. There were more tears, more hugs, and more laughter. There were "thank God" prayers and "best wishes" from everyone. It was overwhelming.

After the doctors had cleared them for leaving the hospital, and after the law enforcement officials had finished all of their official duties, Larry and Connie Van Oosten were finally headed home. It was midday on Thursday, February 9, well over 48 hours since the nightmare had begun at 7:00 a.m. on Tuesday, February 7. Jeff and Amy loaded their parents into the car.

"Why don't we go to my house?" Jeff suggested. "You can clean up. We can get you some clothes."

"No," Connie said from the back seat.

"Mom, you don't have to go back to that house," Amy said. "You don't *ever* have to go back to that house if you don't want to." But Connie was resolute.

"He's taken enough from me. He's not taking my house, too. I want to *go home*."

While they had been waiting for them to be officially released, Jeff had called his wife, Terri, with an important request.

"Would you please take somebody with you and just clean up the house?"

Their home had been cleared by the police for entry. It was no longer cordoned off as a crime scene. All the police equipment was gone, and all of the officers except one, who stood outside as an assurance of safety, had left. But the house was a mess.

"Just try to clean up anything you can."

The sun was shining when Larry and Connie returned to their home. Terri, her kids, and their family friend Amy were waiting in the driveway. John would follow later, bringing the other grandchildren. Larry, still without shoes, felt the familiar ground with a new appreciation as they walked inside. They were finally back. After all they had been through, after all their prayers, God had brought them back. It was all too much to take in. Unfathomable. After showers and clean clothes, and after throwing away the blood-stained sheets, the family got to talking.

"What do you want from us? What can we do to help?"

These were the primary questions Amy and Jeff had for their parents. *How does a family process and move on after so much trauma?* The four Van Oostens sat in their dining room trying to figure this out. This was the first of many such conversations. They were uncertain about how to move on, . . . except that they needed to get started. Steps had to be taken in order for the healing process to begin. That morning they discussed home security systems, getting a dog, installing a camera—anything to make Larry and Connie feel safe again. None of what they discussed could truly begin to ease the tension, though. They would all learn later on that the trauma they'd just experienced would take years to overcome, if they would ever overcome it at all. Some wounds need a long time to heal, if they ever do.

How would they answer questions about what had happened? What were the kids ready to hear and comprehend? Would the kids feel safe at Grandma and Grandpa's house any longer?

Ultimately, they decided that the family needed to be together. The grandkids should be with their grandparents and see for themselves that everything was okay. Amy called John and asked him to pick up something for lunch and to bring the kids. There was an impromptu family meal at Grandma and Grandpa's house. To their surprise and joy, the grandkids just jumped right back in. The resiliency of the children proved to be a much-needed balm. No one—*no* one—could break up this happy reunion.

PART II

CHAPTER TEN

GOD IS IN THE DETAILS

The bad news

At the end of most detective stories there is something called the *big reveal*. It's the part of the story when someone shares the missing information that makes everything fall into place. It's when Sherlock Holmes explains to Dr. Watson just how the crime was committed. It's when the villain is unmasked and all that was secret becomes known.

In TV shows the big reveal is portrayed as a rush of relief. Everyone is so happy to know what was really going on. But that's not always how it works in real life. It was a relief for the Van Oostens to know that it was only Chad Schipper who had held them captive, and that they need not fear the retribution of a gang of criminals. But the weeks and months that followed this experience were long and often very emotional. Though the crime was over, and though Schipper was locked in a cell awaiting trial, each revelation of new information about the crime increased stress and heartache for everyone. The evidence clearly showed that Chad Schipper had meticulously planned this attack against

them for at least a year and half. Each new detail only sickened or
dumbfounded them. The big reveal was not a rush of relief but a
steady, compounding stream of sadness.

On top of this, what they had experienced was nothing short
of acute and sustained trauma. The emotional and psychological
stress was severe. Learning to live with the memories of their
experience would prove to be a long road.

Some of the details that were revealed about the crime
included the following:

- Schipper had indeed entered their home in the middle of
  the night, via the basement window, which he broke and
  cut himself upon during entry. He was inside their home
  as they slept for approximately three hours before taking
  them captive.
- There is an old, abandoned house behind the Van Oostens'
  home. The night before the kidnapping Schipper left his
  Caprice in this location. At some point on Tuesday morning,
  after binding the Van Oostens and leaving them in the upstairs
  bedroom, he moved their car to this property and parked his
  Caprice in their garage so he could load them into the trunk.
- While the Van Oostens were in the trunk of the Caprice,
  Schipper replaced his license plates with plates that he'd
  stolen months earlier.[6] The police later determined that the
  replacement plate was taken from a vehicle at the Quad Cities
  International Airport in Rock Island, Illinois. This led the
  police to wonder at the time whether he had left on a flight.
- After he had driven them to Geneseo and locked them
  in the secret room, Schipper returned to the abandoned

property in Erie. He left his Caprice there, then drove the Van Oostens' car (which had still been hidden in the same location) approximately thirty miles away, to the Quad City Airport. At the airport he left their car in long-term parking, conceivably to make it seem as though the Van Oostens had left town. He then hired a taxi to bring him back to the abandoned property so he could retrieve his Caprice.

- Because their son, Jeff, was on a work trip to the state of Washington, his car was also at the Quad City Airport, overlapping with the time his parents' car was in the same lot (Tuesday night into Wednesday afternoon). This was one of the reasons he was treated as a suspect and interrogated so thoroughly. Not only is it common in cases like these for the criminal to be a close family member, but the fact that he had been at the same location where the Van Oostens' car was found seemed suspicious.

- Schipper stole other articles of their clothing that were never given to them during the crime: two pairs of Connie's shoes, a pair of work boots, a pair of Larry's tennis shoes, a winter coat belonging to Connie, and a jacket belonging to Connie. Some of these items were never recovered.

- The reason Schipper spent such a short time getting gas at Kelly's gas station was that there was an off-duty police officer getting gas right next to him.

- Schipper owned multiple properties, which complicated the search for the Van Oostens. FBI agents and police were moving in on properties across three counties.

- Investigators learned that Schipper lived only a few blocks from the home where he was holding the Van Oostens captive. He would lock them in, go to his house, and eat supper as though he were doing nothing criminal, as though it were just another day.

- Even when the FBI found the correct house, they couldn't immediately find Larry and Connie, the secret room being so well hidden.

- Evidence was discovered that Shipper had hired a contractor to create the room where they were held, indicating the long-term planning and expense he had been willing to go through. This raises the question whether this room was meant to be used only once. Did he have plans for further crimes?

- Pages of detailed notes written by Schipper were later recovered, describing his plan, the room, and each other detail of the crime.

- To-do lists were found in Schipper's home in Geneseo: "Get duct tape. Get zip ties. How to avoid detection. How to destroy evidence. Acid?"[7]

Light in the darkness

"So many things had to happen that we didn't know about for us to be found," Larry would say later. "They had to happen in just a certain way. It had to be God's control for us to get out of there alive."

The Van Oostens believe that the circumstances of their discovery were not accidental, but that God was at work throughout the entire ordeal, steadily bringing them home to freedom. What follows is a list of the positive things that happened in order for Schipper to be suspected and the Van Oostens to be found alive:

- Security cameras filmed Schipper at the Quad City Airport on Tuesday, February 7, hiring a taxi—evidence that was used in the case against him.

- It turned out to be a good thing that the first bank teller Connie spoke with on the phone could not give her an accurate accounting of the monies that were available. Schipper's increasing frustration was what made Connie suggest that they just reach out directly to Mark Hanson. This late-night email from Schipper (posing as Larry) was further evidence against him. It also gave Mark Hanson a fuller picture of what was really happening when Connie appeared in the bank, obviously under duress.

- The cameras at the bank had been recently installed and could see farther and more clearly than the previous cameras. It's unlikely that Schipper knew the cameras had been replaced, or that they were powerful enough to capture an image of his car where it was parked a block and a half away.

- Security cameras from Kelly's gas station also captured images of Schipper paying for gas. Police would later confirm that he had stopped at the station to watch the bank and see whether he was being followed. This provided further evidence used in the case against him.

- The experienced officer who was able to track down the information about the owner of the Caprice and of Store Edge LLC was critical in identifying Chad Schipper.

- Chad drove by the Van Oostens' home to cover up evidence he knew was there, including the blood stains and the broken glass. When he passed the house and saw the police vehicles present, he decided to drive past, and his car was seen. It's unknown why he would have done that after a year and a half of careful planning.

- Though Schipper owned multiple properties, the FBI masterfully coordinated with local law enforcement to have multiple teams moving in on each of the locations. It was a coordinated effort that included a number of different agencies cooperating to get the job done.

- At first, Jeff's cellular provider told the police they could ping the phone a total of only three times during his conversation with Connie. However, thanks to the FBI's involvement, they were able to ping the phone many more times, correctly identifying Geneseo as the Van Oostens' location.

- Chad Schipper was an account holder at First Trust and Savings Bank—the same bank used by Larry and Connie—which made it easier for the FBI to track him down.

- Schipper drove by the Van Oostens' home after his car had been identified at the bank and while officers were stationed at the home.

- The cashier's check was found in the house in Geneseo, serving as further proof of his crimes.

- One of the FBI agents who rescued them just happened to have bolt cutters on hand. No one could have known they would be needed.

In addition to these details about the case, other positive pieces of information came to light when the ordeal was over:

- Connie's hairdresser thought the text she received from Chad (who was posing as Connie) was strange.
- Jim's wife, Kathy (who still gets tears in her eyes when she talks about the situation), also suspected something wasn't right because the text Chad sent to cancel the Wednesday coffee didn't sound like Larry at all.
- While neither person guessed there was criminal activity going on, it was reassuring to know that Chad's messages were not received without suspicion of their not being from Connie and Larry.
- Larry and Connie themselves were quickly ruled out as suspects. This was in large part because of a longtime friendship with the Ven Huizen family. Steve Ven Huizen, who is now Rock Island County police captain, and Jeff Ven Huizen, the Rock Island police chief, have known Larry and Connie for years. The Van Oostens are close friends with their parents. His assurances to the investigating officers that Larry and Connie could not have been involved in any way allowed the police to move forward in the investigation more quickly, ultimately finding the real culprit.
- The Chevrolet Caprice Schipper had been driving was on the news and social media, although he never saw this. If he had, things may have ended differently.

Understanding the will of God and how he works in people's lives is not something anyone can define or decipher perfectly. Theologians have wrestled with these very topics for centuries.

However, Larry and Connie have no doubt that these were not just random circumstances or accidents. They believe fully that these details are evidence of God's hand working on their behalf throughout the whole ordeal, making sure that they got out alive. They are confident that they have seen Romans 8:28 come to life through this experience. They had an experience that most people will never have. They were able to see God working in real time, exercizing his power and control over all things. From the beginning to the end of their ordeal, they can look back and see how he intervened at various times to ensure the outcome he desired, not the evil outcome Schipper had methodically planned. They have greater awareness of how dependent they are on him. All of these events happened over two to three days, and they are easily able to see God in every detail. Many of the trials people face every day aren't over that quickly, but the Van Oostens believe that it is possible to know for certain that God is there and in total control of any situation:

> "And we know that in all things God works for the good of those who love him, who have been called according to his purpose." (Romans 8:28)

These details, however, still leave lingering pain. Amy now carries guilt with her about the phone calls with her mom on Tuesday and Wednesday. She would say later, "I'd talked with her, but I couldn't tell. *I couldn't tell* she was distressed or that something was wrong. Why? Why couldn't I tell something was wrong?"

Like many others in tightknit families, Amy talks with her mom daily. After learning that Connie was being forced to make these calls at gunpoint, Amy would later say to her mother, "You're a good liar. I didn't pick up on anything."

CHAPTER ELEVEN

MANY FACES

February 2017–April 2019
Awaiting sentencing

The Van Oostens never saw the face of Chad Schipper when he forced them from their home at gunpoint. He went to great lengths to keep his identity hidden throughout his crime. At different times he wore a mask, sunglasses, a hat, and a wig. He used a voice modulator and avoided speaking when it wasn't necessary. Through the constant threat of violence, he ensured that they looked at him as little as possible.

Discovering the identity of their captor was a complete shock. How could this man whom they'd known since he was a child do these terrible things to them? They'd gone to church with him and his family for years. They had been his Sunday school teachers, were involved with him in youth group, and interacted again with him later in a young adult class. When his children were born, the Van Oostens would stop by his house to drop off gifts. They didn't know it at the time, but one of the homes they visited years earlier was the very one where they would one day be held captive.

How could he act as though they didn't know him? How could he play such a malicious role with people who had known him as a child and watched him grow up? These are questions that may never have a satisfying answer.

Chad Schipper was arrested on Thursday, February 9, 2017. The following Monday he had his first of many court appearances. On that same day the *Quad-City Times* reported the following:

> Chad C. Schipper, 40, faces charges of home invasion and three counts of aggravated kidnapping.
>
> A preliminary hearing is scheduled for Feb. 27, according to online court records. He remains in the Whiteside County Jail on $1 million bond . . .
>
> The charges all are a Class X felony punishable by six to 30 years in prison.[8]

Schipper was not sentenced until April 2019, two years and two months after his arrest. During this time period Schipper began to play other roles.

In June 2018 the Van Oostens received the first of a series of four disturbing letters written by Schipper. While he was awaiting his sentencing, Schipper became aware of two inmates who were about to be released. He wrote the four letters and gave them to the inmates with instructions to mail them to the Van Oostens from an address outside the jail. In this way the postmark could not be traced back to Schipper himself. He promised the accomplices payment for their troubles.

In the letters, Schipper assumed different personas. The names he used changed, as did the style of writing. He created two fictional lives in an effort to pull his victims into an emotional, manipulative story.

In the first two letters Schipper posed as one "Elouisa Mae," an elderly Southern woman who'd supposedly had her home invaded and her life threatened, similarly to the way Schipper had threatened the Van Oostens. But through the supposed prompting of God, "Elouisa Mae" chose to forgive her one-time captor, "Lewis." Here is an excerpt from the letter, which Connie read alone on her porch after receiving it. The tears fell as she read, not yet realizing that it was really from Schipper, again trying to take control of their lives:

I KNOW THAT WE DON'T KNOW EACH OTHER, BUT I HAVE BEEN PRAYIN FOR YOU AND YOUR FAMILY EVER SINCE I HEARD WHAT HAPPENED, I'M NOT TRYING TO BRING UP MEMORIES THAT YOU WOULD RATHER BE FORGETTIN, BUT I JUST HAD TO REACH OUT TO YOU ALL.

In one letter "Elouisa Mae" reported that she had argued successfully for "Lewis" to receive an early release for his crimes, and in an unbelievable turn of events the state's attorney who was prosecuting him ended up in prison instead. After "Lewis" was released, he purportedly went on to become a beloved minister who saved "many souls," as well as a family man with many grandchildren, one of whom became "a missionary overseas."

In these letters Schipper described a scenario that might have caused the state's attorney to give him only a three-year sentence if both "Elouisa Mae" and the Van Oostens were to reach out on his behalf. In character as "Elouisa Mae," Schipper wrote (in capitalized, block letters):

MAYBE YOU SHOULD THINK ABOUT VISITING CHAD AND SEE WHO HE REALLY IS BEFORE SENTENCING HIM. I AM SO GLAD THAT I VISITED LEWIS. I BELIEVE IT MAY HELP YOU AND HIM. DON'T LET ANYONE TELL YOU THAT YOU CAN'T DO THIS. AS ALWAYS PRAY TO THE LORD FOR GUIDANCE ON WHAT YOU SHOULD DO. HE WILL TELL YOU. I PRAY YOU WILL TELL THE STATES ATTORNEY TO ACCEPT THIS DEAL [the three-year sentence]. TELL HIM YOU JUST WANT IT OVER WITH. TELL HIM WHATEVER THE LORD BRINGS TO YOUR HEART. I PRAY YOU WILL GIVE CHAD A CHANCE TO RESTORE HIS LIFE.

. . . PLEASE DO IT WHOLEHEARTEDLY, AND DON'T GIVE UP. THE LORD WILL BE WITH YOU EVERY STEP OF THE WAY.

The story Schipper wove in these two letters was emotionally and spiritually coercive. It included tear-jerking details about the untimely death of a child, as well as the promise of spiritual directions and blessings from God. Passages from the Bible were quoted in a blatant attempt to elicit guilt on the part of the readers. Schipper insinuated that spiritual peace would come to Larry and Connie, as it supposedly had for his fictional characters, if they would follow his instructions.

The fictional account of "Lewis's" life after prison was meant to be analogous to Schipper's. It constituted a false promise of all Schipper would do with his life if the Van Oostens would only help him escape a long prison sentence.

The Van Oostens received the letters at their home, and at first Connie read them with great concern for "Elouisa Mae," wondering all the while how this person could know so much about the case. It was Larry who immediately felt suspicions. Jeff agreed. "Something isn't right about this," he said. "You've got to call the police."

After turning over the letters, the police traced the postmark back to a residence in Rockford, Illinois. There they confiscated the remaining two letters, written in the voice of "Elouisa Mae's" fictional daughter and further imploring the Van Oostens to argue for leniency for Schipper.

A search was made of Schipper's cell, and hand-written, detailed plans to escape the jail were found.

Meanwhile, in court, Schipper was filing court motions in an attempt to get a more lenient punishment than what would fit his crimes. There were postponements and delays, month after month.[9] Every delay felt like another injustice for Connie and

Larry. There were times when they felt despair and experienced spiritual attacks.

"You know that God is in control, even though the wait seems endless," Larry said. "The pretrials are time that shows your weakness."

Occasionally the delays seemed absurd. During one court appearance, for another case, Schipper purportedly had a fainting spell in the shower just prior to his appearance in court. Court was delayed, and he was taken by police guard to a local hospital, only to be released soon afterward.

The Van Oostens learned the at once beautiful and terribly difficult reality of the American judicial system. Per the Constitution, defendants are innocent until proven guilty. This is a wonderful protection for those wrongly accused. However, in a case like this one, where there is a mountain of evidence against the accused, it's incredibly taxing on the victims. It can feel as though everyone is concerned only about the guilty party.

In a later interview, Whiteside County Sheriff John Booker would say, "One of the huge things [about the judicial system]— and it's taken me a long time to realize this—is that everyone is *presumed innocent*. So, the whole time he's sitting there [in court] he's an innocent man, technically. He has the rights of an innocent man. Until a person goes to trial, they are one hundred percent an innocent person. Although this was one of the best, [most] solid cases we ever had, he was [presumed] innocent."

Though Schipper confessed to the crime at the scene of his car crash, that was not considered a confession.

"The only guilty plea is what he says in front of a judge," Sheriff Booker said. "Everything we get is more evidence against him. The room he built, the statement he made [at the scene of the crash], that's all evidence to present in front of a judge. Statements don't mean he's guilty. Nothing is the final say until he's in a courtroom and the judge accepts a plea of guilty or he's found guilty in court. And that's the hardest thing [for victims]."

It is plain to see that Schipper's attempted manipulation of the Van Oostens was surreal and profound. In his letters he tried to convince them to argue for lenient sentencing on his behalf. The same man who had held them at gunpoint and threatened to kill them and their family tried to trick them into reducing the punishment for his crimes. The same man who would not show his face to people who really knew him created more personas, further attempting to manipulate by burying his true identity.

At the same time, Connie and Larry were forced to watch as his rights were protected through a prolonged process of pretrials and court motions. It was a long, painful education on the American judicial system.

In one of the letters Schipper wrote of himself:

CHAD IS NOT EVIL. HE DID EVIL THINGS, BUT HE IS NOT EVIL.

CHAPTER TWELVE

A WOLF IN SHEEP'S CLOTHING

April 3, 2019
Whiteside County Courtroom

After two years of pretrial hearings, with postponements coming month after month, as well as six and a half hours of further court proceedings, Schipper finally received his sentence. The local ABC affiliate WQAD 8 ran a story online and on the air with the headline, "Geneseo man accused of kidnapping Erie couple sentenced to life in prison."[10] An excerpt from the report is as follows:

> Schipper—already pled guilty—appeared in court on Wednesday for his jail sentence as the Van Oostens sat inside the Whiteside County Courtroom once again seeing the man who held them hostage back in 2017 . . .
>
> "This case had a great impact on the Van Oostens," says State's Attorney Terry Costello. "They got a life sentence, no matter what you do with Chad Schipper today, the Van Oostens got a life sentence. They didn't

113

ask for it, they didn't do anything to get it but they have it."

The Illinois Crime Victims' Bill of Rights is posted on the website for the attorney general for the state of Illinois.[11] Among these rights is "the right to be heard at any post-arraignment court proceeding in which a right of the victim is at issue and any court proceeding involving a post-arraignment release decision, plea or sentencing."

The Van Oostens exercised these rights by reading victim impact statements. These statements allow victims to describe the emotional toll of the crime they suffered to the court. Here's an excerpt from Connie's statement, which she read in court on the day of Schipper's sentencing.

> If you asked me today what I remember about that day I could remember every detail because I relive it almost every day—the trunk of the car, the red lights in each corner of the room he kept us in to monitor everything we did, the room [where] he took me to call my family while he held a gun on me.
>
> Since we have been home, our lives have changed from a fairly easy-going lifestyle to one based wholly on security. I am constantly afraid, I am cautious about everything. Nighttime is the worst, the feeling of being safe in our home was taken from us. I also have a difficult time traveling, which was never the case before.

There is another reason for the constant fear. Last summer I went to the mailbox and there was a letter addressed to Larry and I from a person in Rockford. This woman explained how she had gone through something similar in her life and wanted to reach out to us. A week later another letter came from the same woman—this one was 8 pages long—and wanted us to go see Chad and forgive him. We turned them over to the sheriff's department and found out that they came from Chad, and they found two more letters . . .

This is the person that he is. He wants to manipulate people to get what he wants. He wanted us to feel sorry for him and see that he received a light sentence.

But what about us? We suffer every day for what he has done. I live in fear that he is going to continue to reach out to us. He was after money and when he got what he wanted he was going to kill us. What about the next person? Or the people that he has already stolen from? He is not going to stop.

Our family lived in fear those two days that we might never come home. Chad kidnapped us and held us for those two days. His plan was to take everything from us, even our lives . . . He is a manipulator. He tried to take our money by playing a part as a terrorist whose job it was to go across the country kidnapping people and then turning over all their money to a corporation. If not, his only daughter would be hurt. He said he worked for some very bad people. He also tried to manipulate us through letters written by a lady by the name of "Elouisa Mae," looking for sympathy from us to help Chad. He played the part well—the second letter was even more frightening . . . This shows what lengths he will go to.

Connie ended her statement with the following:

To try and explain how this has affected our lives: I hope by hearing just a small part of what we went through— the gun, the room especially designed for this purpose, the handles on the wall, the handcuffs, the duct tape and the threat to our lives and our family—these are reasons that I'm living in constant fear and am unable to do so many of the everyday things I did in the past, and why some days I'm not able to function at all. This is not the life we had hoped and planned for. Chad will tell you stories, and that is exactly what they are, stories, to play on your sympathies. But please remember he played a part when he took us, and he played a part when he wrote those frightening letters. Please don't allow him to hurt anyone else.

Larry also read a victim impact statement in court. He touched on the things that most men would struggle with—the inability to protect one's spouse, the continued fear for the safety of one's family, the feeling of powerlessness. He said,

> This is not about revenge its to keep him from doing this to others. It haunts me that I couldn't protect Connie more than I did. I keep going over it all the time to see if I could have gotten to him. To see [Connie] degraded the way she was, and having a gun aimed at her constantly is hard to deal with, makes me feel like I failed her . . .
>
> The hardest thing for me to see is how this has changed my wife. She was a sales rep and traveled all over Iowa and Illinois with friends and clients everywhere, she would leave on her own and think nothing of it. Now she does not want to leave home and is uncomfortable in crowds because of what this criminal has done.
>
> To know that this person who we saw grow up, who we taught in Sunday School and who we delivered baby gifts to was going to kill us for money is hard to even imagine.
>
> This whole thing started approx. three and a half years ago when he came to our house claiming to be a financial consultant. Shortly after his visit he started asking me for money, he was obsessed with buying a large house and became very persistent in his efforts, this went on for a long time. Finally, I told him no, when he asked why I told him he had a very poor business

plan and that it was highly unethical for him to ask for money after acting as a financial advisor. That's when he started this plan to get whatever money he could.

He planned for one and a half years. He built a concrete cell costing thousands of dollars to keep us in and then planned to kill us after he got what he could and still to this day shows no remorse. This cell was not for a one-time use. If he had gotten away with this, he would continue to use it and eventually someone would be killed.

Our biggest fear is that this potential killer will get out of prison and be physically capable of harming someone else. He threatened my family and I don't want my kids or grandkids looking over their shoulders. If he is free to do something to them or anyone else he absolutely will. He planned this for years. He will continue to plan while he is in prison. Just while he has been in Morrison, he has written an escape plan and found a way to reach us through the mail.

I'm not sure how he is going to portray himself, he's been an actor all of his life and his intent is evil. I know he needs to be locked away for a long time so he can't harm anyone else.

Schipper's crimes may have been against Larry and Connie directly, but the entire family was harmed and violated. Amy's victim impact statement included the following:

He turned my life upside down, he turned my mom's life upside down, my dad's life, my brother's life, my husband, my daughter, my son, my sister-in-law, my nieces, my nephew, my 90-year-old grandmother, my aunts, my uncles, my cousins, the town of Erie no longer felt safe, the town of Geneseo no longer felt safe and the countless other people he terrified, including his own family. What kind of person does this? My mom and dad will never be the same people that they were. He took their security, their trust in people. He took my parents away from me.

Amy's impact statement goes on to describe the personal toll Schipper's crimes took on her. Her comments provide insight into the enormous strain trauma puts on people, even those who are not at the center of a traumatic event. Her comments also highlight how interconnected families are. When one person is in pain, everyone is in pain to some degree.

We are now two years away from this and we are all still struggling. I am still struggling.

I watch [my parents] struggle every day . . .

I struggle with how much to tell my children. They have questions, but I want to protect them from this evil. They want to know if their grandparents are ok. They want to know if I'm ok . . . How do I comfort them and protect them when I have the same worries? How do I look them in the eyes and tell them everything is going to be ok, when their innocence has been broken by this horrible evil that has happened to our family?

. . . He may say that he just needed money, but he took so much more than that. He stole our safety, he stole our security, he stole our kids' innocence, he stole my confidence and he stole my faith in mankind.

Please don't let him do this to anyone else. I wouldn't wish this on anyone.

Jeff's statement is also a testimony of God's power in an awful circumstance, as well as a reminder of the hardship we may have to endure.

On the afternoon that I received a phone call that my parents were being held against their will, I immediately went to their house and waited for the police. While waiting I knelt on the ground in their driveway and prayed for their safety. By the grace of God this gave me the clarity to be calm.

I talked to my mother while the police tried to get the location of her phone. I had to talk to my mother like I had no idea he was listening. I had to listen to her lie to me so he wouldn't harm her or my father. He would not let me talk to my father, who I talk to daily. I had to pretend that there was nothing wrong when I knew there was.

This testimony reveals that, even when God is at work, life is not always easy. Jeff's role in the search for Connie and Larry was critical, but also incredibly hard for any son to have to endure.

Near the end of his statement, Jeff asked the court to consider chilling questions about Schipper's capabilities. These questions point to the incredible need victims of crime have for justice.

> Chad had threatened, [that] if they did not do what he said, their children and grandchildren would be harmed. Well, they did not do what he said. Am I in danger? Are my children in danger? Is my sister, and her family in danger? If he is willing to take years to plan how to do this to my parents, is he willing to spend years in prison fulfilling his promise? What will he be capable of if he gets out?

Chad C. Schipper is now serving four sentences in Menard Correctional Facility in southwestern Illinois. He was sentenced for sixty years for each of two counts of aggravated kidnapping with a concealed identity, sixty years for one count of home invasion with a dangerous weapon, and eight years for one count of theft.[12]

"The sentencing was kind of a rollercoaster," Connie said later. "One minute the judge would say something like, 'Well, it's his first offense.' Then a few minutes later he would say something else. Finally, the judge called him "a wolf in sheep's clothing." I believe he saw this through our impact statements, and even through Chad himself."

Among the evidence of Chad's crimes, and his confession, the letters demonstrated the dangerous depths to which he would descend in order to manipulate and control others.

The sentencing wasn't the end of the story. Some of the nagging questions around this case were "why" questions. Why the Van Oostens? And if Schipper had been planning the crime for so long, why choose to act on that particular day? The *Sauk Valley News* included the following in their story about his sentencing, which helps answer these questions:

> Although he had been planning the crime for a year and a half, Schipper "pulled the trigger" when he did because he was about to be discovered committing another crime, Costello said. As her financial adviser, he had taken $308,000 from his grandmother; his uncle found out and threatened to sue.
>
> Schipper wrote him a cashier's check to cover the theft just days before, and it was about to bounce, Costello said. "He was desperate to act to cover that check."

The article continued:

> Today's sentence is by no means the end of Schipper's legal troubles.
>
> On Nov. 13, he was charged with theft in the new case, accused of obtaining "unauthorized control" over more than $100,000 but less than $500,000 in currency . . .

He faces 4 to 15 years in prison if convicted. He has a pretrial hearing on July 9.[13]

There were some unexpected blessings at the sentencing. On that final day in court all six of the FBI agents who had rescued the Van Oostens from Schipper's house came to hear the sentencing. It had been over two years, and all of them lived hours away in Chicago and Rockford, Illinois, yet there they all were. They lined up in the chairs behind the table where Schipper sat, clearly sending a silent message to the one-time kidnapper.

Even though they were in plain clothes, the Van Oostens recognized them right away. The memories came back quickly when the six officers approached them during a break in the proceedings.

"Do you remember us?" one of the agents asked with a smile.

"Oh! You *guys*!" Connie exclaimed.

"We wouldn't be anywhere else!"

The agents stayed the whole day. After court was adjourned, the Van Oostens were escorted to the law library in the courthouse. The six agents followed for a round of congratulatory hugs. Amid the celebration Connie and Larry learned that on the day they were rescued, these six agents—after everything was over—had gone out for breakfast and a shot. Now, every year on that same date, these agents reunite for another hot breakfast and shots. They celebrate the day they were able to find two missing kidnapping victims, alive and relatively unharmed, and also catch the man responsible.

Most kidnapping stories don't end this way. The FBI agents know this all too well and choose to honor the day that the story ended differently.

In an interview, Sheriff John Booker reflected on the case:[14]

This was absolutely the most detailed and unique investigation [I've encountered]—and I've been doing this almost thirty years. We realized immediately that this was something a lot more than the sheriff's office had ever seen. We had fabulous leadership with the FBI. It was unbelievable the knowledge that these FBI guys had that they brought to us.

I think we absolutely saved these people's lives. He threatened to kill them all the time. I think that would have been the outcome, had we not caught him so quick. The FBI believed the same as well.

It was excellent police work with all the agencies working together. Not one agency could've done this themselves. We were in the right place at the right time.

Amy called the carpet layer on Friday, February 10, the day after her parents returned home. She wanted to apologize for giving the FBI his name. She simply couldn't hold it in any longer.

"I am *so* sorry. I never thought you could do any of this, but I had to tell them you were in the house."

"Please stop," he said warmly. "I would do it all over again. I would let them in my house. I would let them pull me out into the street again to help you find your mom and dad."

The fear and terror of the previous days were overwhelming. To get everything out in the open was a balm against everyone's hurt and pain.

"I've never been a praying man," he said. "But I prayed for them that night."

CHAPTER THIRTEEN

THE ROAD AHEAD

"Never will I leave you; never will I forsake you."

HEBREWS 13:5

This chapter contains reflections from Larry and Connie:

The story you've just read is something we could have never anticipated. It's an experience we didn't ask for and one that we wouldn't wish upon anyone. As you read in our victim impact statements, we were not the only ones affected by these crimes. There was a ripple effect of pain through our family and community. We have never experienced something so devastating and destructive before. It is like a wound that leaves a scar, but never fully heals. So many were hurt by this too, not only our family but Schipper's family too.

We were approached by the media for interviews after these events first occurred. At the time, we chose not to speak to them.

We're just regular people who try to lead quiet lives. We didn't want to be in the spotlight.

So why tell our story now? Second Corinthians 1:4 tells us that Jesus comforts us in all our troubles so that we can comfort those in any trouble with the comfort we ourselves have received from God. We sincerely want to do that.

We knew from the beginning that something good could and should come out of all of this. But it took a while to feel ready. It was then that God put Russ Holesinger in our path; he felt strongly that our story needed to be told. Through his contacts and efforts, we are able to bring our story to light. After time started to pass and we were able to begin talking about the trauma we'd experienced, we began to realize we shouldn't keep this story to ourselves any longer. While we were held captive, Larry read Romans 8:28 and prayed that something good would come of this. As we started to talk with friends and family about what had happened, we saw how God could use our story to speak to the hearts of others. We wondered if others would feel like the carpet layer did, willing to talk with God in prayer because of our story.

Is his prayer an example of the good that could come out of this experience? We think it might be.

There's a story in the Bible often called "Joseph and the Coat of Man Colors." Joseph was one of 12 sons to a man named Israel, the patriarch of the nation Israel. Joseph was favored by his father and given an extravagant gift, which ignited white-hot jealousy in his older brothers. They surprised Joseph one day, as they were out tending their flocks of sheep, and far from their home and their father. They beat him, threw him in a pit, and eventually sold him as a slave to passing travelers. His brothers then deceived their father, leading Israel to believe that Joseph had been killed by a wild animal. Meanwhile, Joseph ended up in Egypt, alone in a land completely foreign to him.

Yet the Bible tells us that even though Joseph had suffered so much injustice and cruelty, "the Lord was with Joseph and he prospered."[15] Everything was taken from Joseph, including his dignity and his freedom. At one point he was even falsely accused of rape and thrown in the pharaoh's prison. But still, "the Lord was with him."[16]

Later in Joseph's story he was freed from prison and worked his way to a high rank among the Egyptian people. A famine brought his brothers to Egypt years later. Joseph had the power to withhold the grain they needed. He even had the power to imprison them for what they had done to him. He could have taken revenge. But, instead, he said to them, "But as for you, you meant evil against me; but God meant it for good, in order to bring it about as it is this day, to save many people alive." Genesis 50:20 NKJV)

We had no idea what awaited us as we descended into that dark room beneath the closet. We were locked in a prison like Joseph was. Everything was taken from Joseph, including his freedom. (Sounds familiar.) But he was eventually freed and literally went from a pit to a palace. After he found freedom, and after he had all the power and clout he could have wanted, he said his famous words, words that we would like to echo in our own way: *Chad Schipper may have meant evil against us, but God meant it for good, in order to save many people.*

Could God use our story for good somehow? Like the friend we mentioned earlier, would other people consider reaching out to God if they heard our story and knew what he had done for us? We started to feel that telling others our story was something God wanted us to do, even if we didn't always want to. There are days when it would be much easier to stay on the farm and not talk about it at all.

This experience has not given us the answer to every spiritual riddle. But this experience did not make us want to leave our faith, either. In fact, it has deepened our dependence upon God and increased our trust in him. He's the reason we are alive to tell the story.

As frightened as we were, we knew that we were ready to die. We knew beyond the shadow of a doubt that if either of us died, that person would be in heaven with our Savior, Jesus. We were afraid at times, sure. But we weren't afraid of death; it holds no power over those who put their faith in Jesus. In a very real sense, Chad's gun couldn't hurt us. Do you have this certainty in your life? Do you know where you're headed when you die? If you don't and you want the same peace, please don't wait—act now. Give Jesus a chance. Let Him know what's in your heart.

What God promises

Jesus, who you've probably pictured as a baby lying in a manger scene at Christmastime, or as the broken man hanging in a loincloth on a cross, is *a real person*. He claimed to be the Son of God, and by his miracles and his teaching he proved that he was indeed who he claimed to be. Throughout his life on earth, Jesus amassed disciples, far from perfect men and women—fishermen, tax collectors, and prostitutes—who literally followed him from village to village, listening to him teach and modeling their lives after his. As he taught, he began to tell them about a personal sacrifice he would make:

> From that time on Jesus began to explain to his disciples that he must go to Jerusalem and suffer many things at the hands of the elders, the chief priests and the teachers of the law, and that he must be killed and on the third day be raised to life. (Matthew 16:21)

The Bible contains dramatic accounts of the day Jesus was crucified. Darkness covered the land. Huge curtains in the Jewish temple were torn in half. And even the dead were raised.[17]

But what's more incredible than these miraculous events is that his death paid the debt of our sins and yours, too. The Bible teaches that no human being can ever be good enough, perfect enough, or do all the right things to get to God. We're not capable of that because we're all sinners. Romans 3:23 famously says, "for all have sinned and fall short of the glory of God."

But God provided a way for us to be with him—to have our debt paid—through Jesus's death and resurrection. Jesus was without sin. As God's Son, he was the only perfect human being. When he willingly gave up his life, he carried everyone's sin on his shoulders with him. He paid the debt that only he could pay—including ours and yours. Out of love, Jesus made a way for sinners like us to get to God. You can know this for certain! God loves you. It doesn't matter what you've done or how far you have fallen—he loves you no matter what and wants you in heaven with him for eternity. The only way for this to happen is through faith in Jesus Christ. Right now, if Chad asked for forgiveness and truly meant it—and maybe he has—we would celebrate that. God would forgive him and forget all about his sins. It's hard, if not impossible, for us to understand that kind of love, but it is real, and you can depend on it.

In Romans 6:23 we read, "for the wages of sin is death, *but the gift of God is eternal life in Christ Jesus our Lord*" (emphasis ours).

One of Jesus's disciples, John, wrote these famous words about the death of Jesus:

> For God so loved the world that he gave his one and only Son, that whoever believes in him shall not perish but have eternal life. For God did not send his Son into the world to condemn the world, but to save the world through him. (John 3:16–17)

As you read our story, did you feel something indescribable in your heart? Do you want the peace we had when we thought we were going to die?

Did you feel as though God were somehow reaching out to you, or speaking to you?

Did you feel convicted of sin in your life?

If you could, would you begin a relationship with God right now?

If you answered yes to any of these questions, then we want to invite you to pray to God *right now*. Please don't wait! That inner sense of conviction—that awareness of God's voice—is the Spirit of God reaching out to you. The Bible is full of accounts of the Spirit speaking to people in miraculous ways. That sense you have inside may be another miracle. If you answered yes to any of these questions, then please pray the following prayer. You don't have to do this in any special way; you don't have to clean up your life before you pray. He wants you just the way you are. You can say these words out loud or in your head. All that is important is that these words *come from you heart*:

Dear Lord,

I am a sinner. I know this, and I know that I cannot overcome my sin on my own. I don't have the power. But I believe that you do, and I want you to be the Lord of my life. Please forgive me for the things I've done and help me to follow you from this day forward.

Amen.

Next steps

If you prayed this prayer, then tell someone about it! Find someone you trust and share your story with them. Tell them about why you decided to pray this prayer. Tell them what was going on in your heart and mind. If this person is a follower of God, they will be overjoyed. If they're not a follower of God, at least someone you trust will know about this spiritual decision.

After that we encourage you to find a community of other people who love God. Find people who are authentic, not judgmental, and helpful guides in the next steps of your new walk with Jesus. We are all sinners. Even after committing to follow God in prayer, you will find yourself sinning again. God's enemy, Satan, is never happy when someone makes a decision for Christ. He may attack your heart and mind now more than ever. However, part of God's grace is his continual presence in your life. Let him help you in your new life and guide you to take the next steps in faith.

Don't be dismayed if tonight, or tomorrow, or five minutes from now you are tempted to sin again. This is to be expected. By praying this prayer, you have declared that you have joined God's side of a spiritual war. (More about this in a minute.) The enemy of God is now your enemy, and he will work against you. The temptation to sin will be with you throughout life. Unfortunately, old habits die really, really hard. But God will forgive you, no matter what. He doesn't expect you to be a perfect Christian. We're not perfect, either. He just wants your heart to be committed to following him in faith and trust.

For hurting Christians

As we have already said, God doesn't promise that being a Christian means that life will always be rosy and sweet. God doesn't promise everything will be perfect. In fact, James, whom most scholars believe to be the half-brother of Jesus, wrote in the book of James, chapter 1:2–4, "Consider it pure joy, my brothers and sisters, whenever you face trials of many kinds, because you know that the testing of your faith produces perseverance. Let perseverance finish its work so that you may be mature and complete, not lacking anything." Notice that James doesn't say *if* you face trials but *when*. We *will* face trials of many different kinds. If we face our trials knowing that God is in control, we will be able to persevere through those difficult times, and this will help us become mature and complete in Christ.

Is this a quick and easy process? Not always. Did we consider our kidnapping to be "pure joy"? Absolutely not. We are still working through some of the feelings we have. However, our faith in God has increased immensely. We know without a doubt that he is absolutely in control of all things and that we can trust him with everything in our lives. If you stop and think about it for a minute, many of the most famous characters in the Bible—all followers of God—endured suffering and hardship.

Abraham and Sarah were infertile, and ashamed of it, for years.

Joseph faced numerous injustices, including being sold as a slave by his own family, falsely accused of rape, and suffering imprisonment.

Moses was taken from his home as a child, then exiled from his adopted home.

Esther had to place her life on the line in order to protect innocent lives.

Daniel was taken from his home by the local authorities for following God, then sentenced to capital punishment and thrown into a dark hole with hungry lions.

Mary, the mother of Jesus, suffered the shame of an out-of-wedlock pregnancy, which was punishable by death in her culture.

Stephen, Peter, Paul, and many of the other early disciples suffered beatings, imprisonment, and death for following Jesus. In fact, all but one of Jesus's apostles (John) were purportedly killed for their faith in Jesus. These men were with Jesus every day for three years. They were eyewitnesses of everything he said and did. They knew he was who he said he was, the Son of God.

Jesus himself was taken into custody under false charges. Tried in a court. Had lies said about him to the arbiter. Then sentenced to beatings and death. And he indeed died.

This list is not meant to discourage you, but rather to confirm that being a follower of God is not always easy!

But why is this the case?

Because there is a spiritual war being waged that sometimes causes us to suffer spiritual, emotional, and physical consequences.

In Ephesians 6:12 we find one of the clearest explanations of spiritual warfare:

> For our struggle is not against flesh and blood, but against the rulers, against the authorities, against the powers of this dark world and against the spiritual forces of evil in the heavenly realms.

We have seen this evil firsthand in the person who kidnapped us. For him to have done the things he did with absolutely no feeling of remorse is hard to understand in any earthly way. We believe he was caught up in a struggle by spiritual forces of evil. Don't let Satan get a foothold in any part of your life—you can see what that did to Chad.

We can't explain to you the finer points of spiritual warfare. As we've said, we don't have all the answers. But we have found that Satan will still fight his war against Christians even *after* they have suffered.

What we went through with Chad Schipper was awful. It has utterly changed our lives. In many ways, that experience will always be with us. Even knowing that Chad was caught, placed in jail, and eventually imprisoned, we still remember all he did to us and feel the war raging against our spirits. Even on the day that he was sentenced, we were not filled with joy. It was a sad event to behold.

Life after this experience has been a constant fight against tides of negativity, anger, and fear that sometimes threaten to drown us. Negativity will eat at you until you are broken down. Time and again as we have processed these events, we have needed to turn back to God and ask him to remind us of the reality of his presence and of our situation. We've had to pray to him the words of Romans 8:28 and Genesis 50:20 and ask him to make something good come out of this situation. We also find great comfort in Jesus's words in John 16:33: "I have told you these things, so that in me you may have peace. In this world you will have trouble. But take heart! I have overcome the world."

We've felt from the beginning that we could not let Satan win. Continually being a victim does no good for anyone. We will not let the evil of Chad Schipper dominate our lives. We believe that God wants more from us and that this whole episode will be used for his glory and honor. We look back and wonder how this could have happened. We realize again that God is in control. We were able to see God working in real time. We were rescued in a matter of days, and God's intervention was obvious. It doesn't always happen this way. God's intervention may take years. We may not even see results until we are in heaven. But we can be assured that he is always there working for our good.

This might be surprising. After all, who would want to trust in a God who allows you to be abducted? Who wants to trust a God who allows your lives to be threatened? The lives of your kids and grandkids?

Here's the thing: *God didn't do those things to us.* That was Chad. Not God. God didn't create that situation, but he was there with us. What this experience has taught us is that *no matter what you're facing, God will be with you.* He was with us when we were handcuffed in that room. He was with us when a gun was being pointed at us. He was with us when our lives were threatened, when our family's safety was threatened. He was with us through those sleepless nights. He's there with you, too, in whatever you're facing.

People want to assume that if you become a Christian, everything will just go smoothly. Everything will be rosy, and you'll have no problems. Well, it's one thing to read Bible verses, but you've got to believe them. A trouble-free life isn't what God promises. He doesn't promise to take away every trial or every pain. He doesn't promise to keep us safe all the time. Even God's followers in the Bible were occasionally threatened, beaten, and killed. So, what does he promise? Something better. Eternal life through Jesus Christ, his Son.

Spiritual warfare, healing from deep wounds, recovering from trauma—these are hard, hard things, even for Christians. We have found that it is so important to have a church family you can depend on. The phrase "love God, love others" has been key to our healing. Being a part of a church family allows us to give love and feel loved by other followers of Jesus. This sense of community is so significant for healing.

Being willing to forgive others is also key to the healing process. Matthew 6:14–15 says, "For if you forgive other people when they sin against you, your heavenly Father will also forgive you. But if you do not forgive men their sins your Father will not forgive your sins." These are words directly from Jesus, so we know that we need to forgive. It's a huge part of the healing process. But how do you do it? We have struggled with this. It certainly doesn't happen right away. There are even times when you think you have finally been able to forgive, and soon afterward you have thoughts that let you know you're not there yet. With God's help and a desire to do his will, you will be able to do what you once thought was impossible. Love for others is so important in your walk with Christ.

We've also found that Christian counseling is so important. If you're hurting, then we encourage you to reach out to a licensed Christian counselor and find an encouraging community of believers. Spiritual warfare is not a war to fight alone. Not only is the Spirit of God with you, as he was with us, but other believers, trustworthy counselors, should be with you, too. (Seeking a counselor shows strength and determination to heal—it's nothing to be ashamed of; we have a very wise Christian counselor who has helped us through many of our struggles.) If you know someone who is hurting, simply reach out. If you are struggling, it's okay. It's okay because we're human, weak, and totally dependent on God. He knows this about us and still loves us. We are no different. It's been four years since all of this happened, and we still struggle and often fail. The last thing we want is for anyone reading this book to come away with the idea that we were saved from death and that now we are these perfect Christians with all the answers. Nothing could be farther from the truth.

We want to honor the Lord. Our lives, and especially this story, is all about *him*, not us. You've just read about some remarkable people—the detectives; the FBI agents; Mark and Patty and the other bank personnel; and our children, Amy and Jeff. You've also read about one very lost, evil man. But the main character of this story is God. He was with us every step of the way. He's with us now, on both the good days and the bad days. He reminds us of that indescribable peace that carried us through and offers us more with each prayer, each day of faith in him.

Think back in the story to that moment before we were rescued by the FBI. We were convinced we wouldn't live much longer. But we did have a *peace* in knowing where we were headed after death. Did this peace come because of anything we had done, or because we were perfect Christians and did everything right? Absolutely not! It came solely from the grace and mercy offered to sinners like us, from faith and trust in Jesus.

It's true that we felt that peace when we thought our lives on earth were over, and in some ways that has never left us. But our lives are very different now, too. As an example, one night I (Larry) had a 7:00 p.m. meeting that lasted almost an hour. When I returned home, I could tell that something was very wrong. While I was gone, the power had gone out. I found Connie in a chair. She had been crying and was still shaking in fear. This was never her, but it is now. This is just an example of how different things are for both of us, even as we trust God each day.

We have put our faith in Jesus. He is the God who saved Joseph from slavery and freed him from Pharaoh's prison. He is the God who promises his followers eternity in heaven after they die. He is also the God who can work through detectives, FBI agents, and family members to find lost people. He is the God of indescribable peace.

ACKNOWLEDGMENTS

We have found that it's so important to have true and sincere Christian friends. They are a precious gift from God. To mention only a few:

Vern and Lonavene, who as soon as they realized there was a problem went to our son's house to help in any way they could—and they did. They have always been there for us.

Jim and Kathy, whom we can go to anytime and talk about what we are dealing with. They truly care. Kathy still gets tears in her eyes when we talk about what happened; she has a caring heart. It's so important to have people like this in your life.

Bart, who was dealing with what turned out to be terminal cancer, showed us his love continually. Even though he was dealing with his own problems, each day he took the time to call, visit, or send a text message to see how we were doing. It's truly humbling to have known someone like Bart: his strength, caring, and love of God, made what we had gone through seem small, and we miss him.

Steve and Jeff Ven Huizen, brothers who are both high-ranking police officers, helped us through the whole process. They were continually there for us anytime we had a question.

Russ Holesinger, whose prayer and encouragement have helped make this book possible.

Our good neighbors Jim and Shelia, who remember us every February 7 and bring over delicious baked goods.

Deb and Leo and family. Their oldest son, Jason, and his wife, Amy, were with Jeff from the very start, helping the family in so many ways, and are still a strong support for them. Wyatt, another son, was a constant during the rescue. They also brought over enough food to feed the whole town, along with hugs and many prayers.

Terry, our minister, at the time spent the whole first night we were missing with our kids and grandkids and has been there for us ever since.

Aaron, our youth minister, was there for us and still is; he and Larry talk often.

Michelle Snyder, who gave us great insight and helped us write this book. Also, her family near and far praying and keeping in contact with us through this devastating ordeal.

As we have been writing this book, our country is going through a time when our police, those who serve and protect, are being treated unfairly. This experience has given us a deep, personal respect for every law enforcement agency.

Our Whiteside County Sheriff's Department was amazing. Everything was done professionally and with concern for our wellbeing. The care they showed us is something we will always remember.

When our detective presented the evidence in court, he never missed a beat. The state's attorney did a masterful job in prosecuting the case, and our advocate throughout the process was so kind and considerate in keeping us informed. We thank you all.

The concern and support of the FBI have been overwhelming. From the day they rescued us to the day of the sentencing, they were there.

There are too many people from church and our community to mention. We could go on and on. We received an outpouring of love from our church, through calls, visits, cards, and food.

We remember one visitor named Kathy who normally would have the right words to say for any occasion. But when she came to our house she just stood there, unable to speak. That said it all. You don't always have to say the right thing—just let people know you care.

Our small community was amazing. We received hugs and well wishes every time we went out. All were very much appreciated. Thank you so much. "Love God. Love others."

—Larry and Connie Van Oosten

This book was written during the summer and fall of 2020. I owe an enormous debt to Larry and Connie Van Oosten, who spent hours with me on the phone, telling me their story and answering my endless questions. They opened up their hearts and relived traumatic memories to tell this story. They did so during a trying time of great stress in our culture, too. I only hope I've been able to adequately capture their quiet strength and good humor in these pages.

I also want to thank Amy, Jeff, Mark Hanson, Patty Hoogheem, and Sheriff John Booker for their time and willingness to be interviewed for this book. Each one added a unique perspective on the events, which served to make the story more colorful and nuanced. Thank you all.

Finally, I want to thank Tim Beals for introducing me to the Van Oostens, my writer's group for their enthusiasm and encouragement, and my family for their support and prayers.

—*A. L. Rogers*

ENDNOTES

1. It was reported that this 911 call was made at 4:45, but multiple interviews indicated that this call was made after the bank was closed for the day, likely at 5:45.

2. They would learn later that, as much as they could, other officers tried to keep Chief Heywaert out of the loop, conceivably because they didn't want his friendship with Jeff to somehow interrupt the investigation.

3. Among those working that night was Service Lieutenant John Booker, who would later be promoted to Sheriff. He served as Incident Command for the case. This role required him to set assignments for the various officers as they came in, working to combine their efforts. Booker's knowledge of the case was critical for the research of this book.

4. As reported by The Quad City Times. https://qctimes.com/news/local/crime-and-courts/arrest-made-in-reported-whiteside-county-abduction/article_cc540995-a694-5296-b152-a4d3b072dbea.html

5. https://qctimes.com/news/local/crime-and-courts/arrest-made-in-reported-whiteside-county-abduction/article_cc540995-a694-5296-b152-a4d3b072dbea.html.

6. https://www.shawlocal.com/2019/04/03/kidnapper-gets-60-years-for-terrorizing-erie-couple/anm4ldh/.

7. https://www.saukvalley.com/2019/04/03/kidnapper-gets-60-years-for-terrorizing-erie-couple/anm4ldh/.

8. "Whiteside abduction suspect appears in court," https://qctimes.com/news/local/crime-and-courts/whiteside-abduction-suspect-appears-in-court/article_9cbbc7ca-611f-52eb-9ed0-da21c18dbce4.html.

9. Public information about the case and the list of numerous pretrial hearings can be found on Judici.com. https://www.judici.com/courts/cases/case_information.jsp?court=IL098015J&ocl=IL098015J,2017CF33,IL098015JL 2017CF33D1.

10. https://www.wqad.com/article/news/local/drone/8-in-the-air/geneseo-man-accused-of-kidnapping-erie-couple-sentenced-to-life-in-prison/526-7da4e1b5-fadf-42e7-b22d-2385061329c1 Regarding Schipper's plea, Saul Valley news reported the following: "Schipper pleaded guilty Nov. 14 to two counts of aggravated kidnapping and home invasion. Fourteen other charges, including six other aggravated kidnapping charges, theft, two counts of armed violence, two counts of aggravated battery and two counts of aggravated unlawful restraint, were dismissed as part of his plea agreement." https://www.saukvalley.com/2019/04/03/kidnapper-gets-60-years-for-terrorizing-erie-couple/anm4ldh/.

11. https://illinoisattorneygeneral.gov/victims/bill_of_rights_poster.pdf.

12. https://www2.illinois.gov/idoc/Offender/Pages/Inmate Search.aspx.

13. https://www.saukvalley.com/2019/04/03/kidnapper-gets-60-years-for-terrorizing-erie-couple/anm4ldh/.

14. Phone interview with Sheriff Booker conducted by A. L. Rogers on September 9, 2020.

15. Genesis 39:2, New International Version.

16. Genesis 39:20–21.

17. Matthew 27:50–54.